*The Jewish
Pleasure Principle*

The Jewish
Pleasure Principle

Rabbi Reuven P. Bulka, Ph.D.

Rabbi, Congregation Machzikei Hadas, Ottawa
Editor, *Journal of Psychology and Judaism*

HUMAN SCIENCES PRESS, INC.
72 FIFTH AVENUE
NEW YORK, N.Y. 10011-8004

Printed in the United States of America
987654321

Library of Congress Cataloging-in-Publication Data

Bulka, Reuven P.
   The Jewish pleasure principle.

   Bibliography: p.
   Includes index.
   1. Pleasure principle (Psychology)—Religious aspects—
Judaism. 2. Asceticism—Judaism. 3. Self-denial.
4. Jewish way of life. I. Title.
BM538.P68B85   1987   296.7'4   86-20839
ISBN 0-89885-328-1

To
Our greatest pleasures:
Yocheved, Shmuel, Rena, Eliezer, and Binyamin

Contents

Acknowledgments

Although this volume was prepared relatively recently, the idea of writing a book on The Jewish Pleasure Principle goes back more than 10 years, when I was invited to give a lecture on this topic to the National Council of Jewish Women in Ottawa. The ideas presented then were more general formulations; the specifics, in theory and in practice, are found in this volume.

From the original presentation, until a short while ago, the idea of the book hibernated on the shelf, while I was busy with other writing endeavors. However, upon suggesting this concept to Norma Fox, editor-in-chief of Human Sciences Press, the hibernation period came to an abrupt end. Norma was excited about the project, and encouraged and persuaded me to write the book. I thank her for her enthusiasm, her persistence, her patience with broken deadlines, her insight, and her congeniality.

In the preparation of this book, as with so many others, I have been helped beyond words by the very dedicated secretaries of Congregation Machzikei Hadas, the synagogue I am privileged to serve as its Rabbi. Blanche Osterer was somehow able to put an original manuscript down on paper from a complicated combination of scribbled pages and garbled dictation, and then played around with the multitude of corrections and revisions until the final draft was ready; all this without a word processor. The book deals with pleasure; but her work in preparing it was anything but a pleasure.

Jean Naemark, the other half of the team, was her usual supportive self, ready to help in any way, including the tracking down of sources. To Blanche and Jean go my heartfelt thanks.

Writing a book about pleasure is much easier when one lives in a pleasant environment. I grew up in a pleasant environment, as did my dear wife Naomi. The ambience for the present work goes back to my dear parents, Rabbi and Mrs. Jacob Bulka, and my dear parents-in-law, George and Sessie Jakobovits. They are, unbeknown to them, significant contributors to this volume.

My wife and I have shared two pleasant environments, our home and our congregational family. The pleasantness of the home is her unique achievement; the pleasantness of the congregation is eloquent testimony to the friendliness, kindness, and understanding of our beloved Congregation Machzikei Hadas. These, together with the goodwill of the Ottawa community, have made our stay there a transcending pleasure. In such an atmosphere, it is easy to write such a book.

The book itself is dedicated to our dear children; Yocheved, Shmuel, Rena, Eliezer, and Binyamin. As much pleasure as we have derived from them, we hope this is merely the harbinger of things to come. Anticipatory pleasure, though it should never be taken for granted, is not merely a hope for the future; it is a present delight.

Reuven P. Bulka
Ottawa, Ontario, Canada

Introduction

One of the most neglected and misunderstood aspects of Judaism is its attitude toward pleasure. Perhaps because Judaism is continually bracketed with Christianity and Islam as one of the "Big Three" religions; perhaps because of the austere image projected by some Jewish religious leaders; or because of a backlash reaction to the "playboy" philosophy apparently prevailing in America; or because of a combination of these and other factors, Judaism is perceived by some as a religion of denial, suspicious of pleasure and demanding withdrawal from the experiences of this world.

This is unfortunate, because the erroneously assumed negative attitude to pleasure has doubtless repelled many from Judaism, at the same time that it has made the religious feel guilty about enjoying life. The attitude toward pleasure is thus closely related to the modern crisis in religion, generally and within the Jewish community.

This book is an attempt to place "the" Judaic attitude to pleasure in proper perspective. While it can hardly be denied that the behavior and attitudes of noteworthy Jewish personalities past and present impose a negative attitude to pleasure, it is nevertheless questionable whether this is indeed the intended norm, or another instance of veering toward the extreme at the expense of the golden mean.

It is almost foolhardy to attempt to explicate "the Jewish position" on pleasure, or on almost any other subject, for that matter. The range of opinion in authentically Jewish sources for practically all philosophical concerns is too wide to pinpoint a universally acceptable point of view that would satisfy all factions.

However, it is practical, even necessary, to extrapolate what could be adopted as the golden mean position,[1] formulating a Judaic stance toward pleasure fully consistent with Jewish sources, respectful of Judaic tradition, cognizant of present reality, and hence *livable* by the Jewish people.

Such a position will certainly not excite the hedonists of Jewish persuasion; it is also likely to repel the ascetics, for whom pleasure is almost anathema. It should be pointed out that the hedonist and the ascetic, though probably equidistant from the golden mean, operate from different perspectives. The hedonist affirms this world with all its pleasures, and cares little about any God-given restrictions that put a damper on the experience of pleasure. The ascetic, on the other hand, rejects this worldly pleasure in favor of other worldly, ultimate concerns. For the ascetic, expressing the perceived will of God is the ultimate value. Ironically, this life-style gives the ascetic a sense of fulfillment, or, in a larger sense, pleasure; the pleasure of actualizing God's will. It may therefore be said that the ascetic, too, experiences pleasure, though of a distinctly different sort. In a word, the hedonist's pleasure is the ascetic's pain; the ascetic's pleasure is the hedonist's pain.

I admit at the outset that I work within the confines of a definite bias, the bias toward moderation and reason, which are themselves distinctive features of normative Judaism.[2] Though care will be exercised not to distort Jewish tradition, it is still entirely possible that other individuals, studying the same sources, might select different views as the norms; or interpret statements differently than they may be interpreted in this volume. That, too, is a *pleasure*, that of intellectual stimulation, and surely one closely linked to Jewish *principles*.

The volume itself is comprised of nine chapters. The first spells out the context in which the topic is treated, including a general discussion of the notion of denial.

The second discusses the obligation to maintain one's health, with the third focusing on the avoidance of pain.

Chapter 4 explores the matter of mental pain, or depression, and Judaic norms relative to depression and happiness.

Chapter 5 deals with the experience of pleasure, and chapter 6 with the enjoyment of life, or making life pleasurable for the self and for others.

Chapter 7 elaborates on the pleasures of the palate, and chapter 8 on sensual pleasure.

The concluding chapter puts the observations of the previous chapters into a total perspective.

This volume, as a proposal entirely consistent with Jewish tradition will, it is hoped, be useful not only theoretically, but also practically, by illustrating that the affirmation of pleasure in a meaningful context is a religious value par excellence.

1

The Context

THE DENIAL TRADITION

The majority religions of America, Catholicism and Protestantism, are historical offshoots of Judaism. The branching off started in the first century of the common era, and gained momentum after the destruction of the Temple in Jerusalem in the year 70.[1] Eventually, Christianity became recognized as the official religion of Rome, and later split into denominations, hundreds in number.

Today, more than 1900 years after its humble beginnings, these denominations still retain, in varying degrees, some of the theological baggage they carried at inception. Christianity at its genesis was a sect within Judaism; more precisely, an extremist sect which rejected this-worldly delights along with some of the more salient features of the Judaism of the day, including the primacy of the Temple, the centrality of Jerusalem, and the authenticity of rabbinic law.

The original Christians withdrew from this world, and retreated into a life-style of privation, denial, and ablution, waiting for the great deliverance through their savior, or messiah.

The tradition of denial promulgated by Christianity is evidenced by some basic norms relating to sensual pleasure. Sex was viewed as sinful, the only "excuse" for sex being procreation. The highest virtue of all was to be a eunuch for the kingdom of heaven's sake.[2] The doctrine of the virgin birth was a necessary correlate of this theology. After all, how could their savior be a child born as a result of a sinful act? In the Roman Catholic church, to this day, priests are not allowed to marry.

To the poor, Christianity offered a redemptive hope. They were told by missionizing Christians that as they were deprived in this world, to that degree they would be prosperous in the afterlife. The rich were using up their credits in this world, and thus, rather than be envied, should be pitied. Thus was promulgated the notion of denial in this world for the sake of gratification in the next.[3]

Even though theologians within the denominations have wrestled with some of the notions mentioned here, the general attitude that denial is a higher virtue persists. That it should spill over into a public perception of religion in general as linked to denial, is understandable.

It should also be mentioned that history is replete with stories of fertility cults serving their gods; surely cogent examples of religion as the very reverse of denial. However, most individuals, whether within or outside the religious framework, look upon these cults as anomalies, perhaps precisely because they do not fit into the "accepted" model of religion.

JUDAISM ON DENIAL

Throughout history, Judaic expression has encompassed a wide spectrum. This diversity includes those who withdrew from this world in order to focus entirely on the word of God and the world of God. In a narrow sense, these individuals practiced some form of denial, but usually it was denial of one aspect of life in order to fulfill another.

Thus, for example, Moses, who was married and had children, nevertheless separated from his wife Zipporah when it became obvious that the only way he could lead the Israelites was by devoting his full time and energies to the pressing leadership responsibilities.[4]

Ben Azzai, a leading Talmudic sage in the second century, when confronted with the fact that he was single, admitted to this failing, but pleaded for understanding. "What can I do, my soul yearns for Torah learning," he said.[5]

Moses and Ben Azzai, among others, are exceptions to the norm, either living in special circumstances or possessing particular characteristics that placed them into different parameters of behavior.

In a sense, they are exceptions that prove the rule that under normal circumstances, one is not allowed to withdraw from the delights of this world. The Talmud, the monumental work explicating the Torah (Bible) and applying its principles to everyday existence, thus asserts that in passing from this world and then confronting ultimate judgment, one will be obliged to explain, among other penetrating questions, why one abstained from enjoying the pleasures and delights of this world.[6] In the words of the Talmud, one who is preoccupied with fasting is considered a sinner.[7]

To place the Judaic attitude toward denial in sharp relief, one need only mention that the *first* commandment, "Be fruitful and multiply,"[8] demands sensual pleasure in order to be fulfilled.

Additionally, obligations to enjoy the culinary delights of this earth, whether on the Sabbath and the festivals or other occasions, such as a wedding, circumcision, redemption of the firstborn, the celebration at a child's reaching the age of religious responsibility,[9] or the religious obligation to enjoy new fruits as they appear in season,[10] illustrate the affirmative attitude of Judaism to this-worldly enjoyment.

There are, to be sure, limitations, times and circumstances that demand restraint from indulgence.[11] However, on balance, it can be safely stated that Judaism rejects the notion of denial for denial's sake, even as it recognizes special situations calling for denial. And those special situations do not negate the general affirmation of the obligation to taste the appealing things of this world.

DENIAL AS RELIGION

The pagans of old who brought sacrifices to their gods believed that these offerings were necessary in order to appease, placate, or please their deities. Failure to bring the sacrifices was sure to incur the wrath of a hungry or jealous god.

The idea of sacrifice almost explicit in this behavior expression was that one must make a tangible sacrifice to show fealty to a higher power.

The Israelites, too, adopted the notion of sacrifice,[12] but they rejected the notion that sacrifice was intended or needed to feed a hungry god. Instead, sacrifice became an act of rapprochement in the face of reproach. For those who had not lived up to their responsibilities, or who had committed a sin, whether an individual or a group, the act of sacrifice was a way of drawing closer to God. In fact, the Hebrew word for sacrifice, *korban*, is rooted in the word *karav*, to draw closer.[13]

This drawing closer was perceived as the equal and opposite reaction to dereliction, which at once reflected and caused a further distancing from God. Through offering a sacrifice, be it anything from turtle doves to whole animals,[14] the person, in the sacred ambience of the Temple, was brought closer to the Creator through the resolve to repent from past misdeeds.

In sacrifice, as in religious expression generally, the focus of attention was the individual. It mattered little to God whether a sacrifice was brought; God was conceived as noncorporeal, beyond the need to eat or drink. What was of crucial importance was that the sacrificial act have a lasting, profound impact on the citizen bringing the sacrifice. When, in later times, the prophets railed against sacrifice,[15] it was a complaint leveled not at the form, but at the substance. It had become a purely ritualistic act, devoid of the intended meaning, and thus a religiously empty expression.

Although sacrifice ceased with the destruction of the Temple, at the beginning of the Common Era, the idea of sacrifice continues into the present. In its positive sense, sacrifice as an act of drawing closer has been replaced by prayer as a means of atoning and coming near to God and the Godly.[16] In its negative sense, one finds individuals who see their adherence to commandments as a sacrifice to please God. It is not unusual to find among those who observe the Sabbath or are mindful of religious dietary restrictions (in the popular parlance, they "keep kosher"), those who complain if life does not give them a fair shake. The implicit argument is that since they have sacrificed (read, denied) for the sake of God, it is only fair and just that God reward them in kind, with good health and prosperity.

Then there are those who tend to follow the stricter interpretation of the law, which for them often involves some form of personal stringency, whenever faced with doubt or lack of absolute surety regarding specific norms. The tendency toward strictness is, to some degree, an adoption of the denial "safety valve."[17]

Perhaps the most ubiquitous form of denial, practiced, ironically, by those who would deny themselves practically nothing in their daily pursuits, is the almost universal, and in some respects, scrupulous observance of Yom Kippur, the Day of Atonement. Even those who openly flout the dietary laws or desecrate the Sabbath or festivals manage to find their way to the prayer services on the Day of Atonement, and also to spend the entire 25-hour period abstaining, as prescribed from food and drink.

Why did Yom Kippur merit the distinction of being the most observed of all Jewish practices? Simply passing off this question with the argument that it is only a one-day affair and therefore easily observable, is too facile. There are other one-day affairs, such as Purim, which cannot claim such distinction.

It seems that Yom Kippur fits quite snugly into the notion of religion as denial. For those who have been distant from God and the Godly 364 days of the year, a one-day-a-year denial for the sake of God seems an appropriate appeasement. After all, God cannot be angry if at least once a year people give up their precious time and regular meals; if the people deny themselves for God's sake. The one-day-a-year people do not usually engage in soul-searching or heartfelt repentance, both of which are essentials on Yom Kippur.[18] They see the fasting not as a means toward a transcending confrontation with one's life, but as an end in itself, specifically as a sacrifice of one's daily pleasures on the altar of appeasement; of appeasing God through denial.

The Yom Kippur idea has unfortunately become grossly distorted. Instead of being the day that launches a fresh, unabating commitment, it has become for too many the day that justifies past and future breaches.

The concept of religion as denial, with the attendant distortions, has thus invaded a significant element within Judaic ranks.

THE FAULT WITH DENIAL

Denial as a normative expression is, at once, a distortion of the Godly ideal and the human imperative. Denial conjures up the image of a god who needs to be appeased, even spoon-fed; it postulates a human reality in which all wrongdoing can be wiped away by an act of denial rather than by an act of repentance. Functional acts are usually less demanding or taxing than honest soul-searching.

If purity of heart and sincerity of purpose are present, then any human act consistent with divine dictates is meaningful. Failing such concomitants, any action is a mechanistic response easily replicated by a robot.

The upshot of a life-style that views religious expression as denial is that one develops a negative view of God as a punishing, demanding reality, and a view of life as full of sordid enticements that must be avoided if one's character is to be considered meritorious. Not only is this debilitating on a personal level, in that it encourages a mechanistic, even melancholy attitude toward life; it is also a repugnant model that only serves to discourage people from adhering to traditional norms.

The story is told of two friends who, having sinned together, decided they would visit, in tandem, their local Rabbi, to confess their sin and ask for an appropriate strategy for penance. After hearing the case, the Rabbi recommended they should go about their business for the next week with peas in their shoes. In midweek, the partners in sin met. One was moving about in considerable pain; the other went around as if nothing had changed. The suffering partner angrily accused his counterpart of openly rebelling against a rabbinical charge. The accused partner protested, insisting that he was following the Rabbi's directions to the letter. "Then why are you not in pain if you have peas in your shoes?" he was asked. He replied "I cooked them first."

There is no benefit in walking about with cooked peas; but there is also none in going around with hard peas, unless the pain experienced with every step is a behavior conditioner, reminding the person at every turn to avoid wrong and adhere to what is right.[19] It is only when denial relates to affirming life, when it leads to a more wholesome embrace of life's contingencies, that it can be countenanced as a necessary component of the human endeavor.

The nineteenth century sage Rabbi Israel of Rizhyn once was approached by a young man who wanted to be ordained. To be better informed about the applicant, the sage inquired about his conduct. The aspiring rabbinical candidate replied, "I always dress in white, drink only water, place tacks in my shoes for self-mortification, roll naked in the snow, and receive 40 stripes every day on my bare back." As the candidate was speaking, a white horse entered the yard, drank water, and started rolling in the snow. "See," said the sage, "this creature is white, it drinks only water, has nails in its shoes, rolls in the snow, and receives even more than 40 whips per day. Still it is nothing but a horse!"

The message of this anecdote of course is that subjecting the self to pain is not a value in itself.

Even more instructive is the story attributed to eighteenth century leader, Rabbi Israel Baal Shem Tov, the founder of Hasidism (a unique brand of mysticism involving a group adhering to a charismatic leader), who was once approached by an anxiety-ridden Jew wanting to know how many days he would have to fast in order to atone for a serious sin. Rabbi Israel told him that fasting does not propitiate God's anger, but the joy of reciting Psalms can achieve this end. Say the Psalms with inner rejoicing, and you will be rid of your sin, advised the Rabbi.

Denial, and the melancholy spirit, estrange; the joyous spirit connects to life in its totality.

THE EXCEPTIONS

The Talmud tells of a first century sage named Rabbi Zadok, who fasted for 40 years, taking only water at night. This saint did not fast because he was a charter member of Weight Watchers. His fasting was a perpetual prayer in anticipation of the coming destruction of the Temple. Rabbi Zadok hoped that through his fasting, this great tragedy could be avoided.[20] The length of Rabbi Zadok's "hunger strike" was unusual, but the underlying ethos of his expression was not.

Rabbi Zadok was just one in the long catalogue of saints who subjected themselves to extended privations. The object was not to deny themselves, but to acknowledge the reality around them, the misery and the tragedy; to concentrate one-sidedly on these conditions, never even for the slightest period of time wavering from deep concern, and from entreating God to bring rain, thwart the evildoer, or arrest the plague. Their saintliness inhered in their being oblivious to themselves and totally concerned with the welfare of the community.

The other domain wherein abstinence prevails involves those who may be called "spiritual athletes"; those who go through strenuous exercises in order to attain spiritual excellence. These exercises take the form of intense meditation; in effect, a necessary withdrawal in order to concentrate on the Godly or on a complex Talmudic passage. The original pietists (deeply religious individuals) would meditate for a lengthy period both before and after praying. Before prayer, they would "meditate up" to the spiritual level at which authentic prayer is possible. Following prayer, they would "meditate down" from prayer level to reality. One could hardly call these meditations denial, even though during meditation these pietists were toally removed from the world. Their purpose was not to deny, but to affirm. The focus was not on abstinence; the focus was on spiritual fulfillment.

Similarly, it is related of a great sage of the nineteenth century, Rabbi Hayyim of Brisk, that he once soaked his feet in cold water for 3 days so that he could stay awake and concentrate on explicating a difficult statement of a leading Talmudic commentary.

In another illuminating vignette, Rabbi Elimelekh of Lizhensk, an eighteenth century Hasidic sage, once said that fasting was not an appropriate mode of service. But, he was asked, did not Rabbi Israel himself, the founder of the Hasidic movement, fast for long periods? Rabbi Elimelekh responded that it was true, Rabbi Israel fasted. When he left the house after the Sabbath to meditate, he would take along a sack with six loaves of bread, and water to sustain him during the week in the forest. When he readied himself on Friday for the return home to celebrate the Sabbath, he found to his surprise that the sack held the same amount of bread as when he left. Such fasting is permitted.

In a word, there are occasions or circumstances in which the achievement of an intentional, meaningful goal is enhanced through abstinence. In such situations, one is not even aware of the privation, so pure and single-minded is the purpose of the intent. For the outsider, this seems to be a form of denial. For the insider, there is no conscious perception of denial; only undivided attentiveness to the goal at hand —a precious instance wherein the paradox "by abstaining we obtain" is realized.

UNCONDITIONAL AFFIRMATION

There are those who may argue that the present condition of the world is sufficiently critical to justify denial, and withdrawal from the corruption and immorality of people and governments promoting hate and killing the innocent.

Is such an argument justified? Is this type of reaction a viable and effective response?

This is not the first time in Jewish history in which the crisis cloud of *To be or not to be* hangs over the heads of so many Jews. There is an historical link between the Jews of Israel in the first and second centuries, the Jews of Poland in the Middle Ages, the Jews of Europe in the 1930s and 1940s, and the present plight of Jews in Russia, Iran, Iraq, Syria, etc.

In the postdevastation trauma of the past, many Jews could not cope with the atrocities their people had been subjected to, and left the fold.[22] Others, realizing that giving up only completed the annihilation attempted by the enemy, decided with even greater resolve to rededicate themselves to the unfolding of Jewish destiny. Such people could not help but be despondent when contemplating the fate of their brothers and sisters, but mustered all the fortitude available to them to ensure that despondency not regress into despair, into hopelessness and helplessness.

In the subhuman conditions of the Nazi concentration camps, there were many who despaired of life itself, who saw life as so utterly meaningless in the face of such degradation, that it was not worth fighting or resisting in order to stay alive. Death was a preferable alternative to human life lived on an animal level.

But there were others who resisted, who refused to give in. The resistance took the form of physical combat, in the model of the Warsaw Ghetto uprising; or the form of spiritual resolve to live out Jewish tradition in the obscene conditions of the camps. Those who "celebrated" Passover, stealthily reciting the Haggadah (Passover text) from memory, or who, in the absence of Matzah (unleavened bread), used discarded potato peels from the refuse heap, are prime examples of this type of resistance. They not only observed the Passover ritual; they also poured forth a defiant joy, powerful and resonant far beyond the time and space of the camps.[23]

The spiritual resistance model in the camps is an appropriate lead-in to the contemporary reality. The possible disasters of the present pale in comparison with the all too real catastrophes of the 1930s and 1940s. Yet even then, the heroic model of resistance that combined awareness of reality with hope, however meager, for a future, however uncertain, asserted itself.

The present bleak conditions for many impose a depressing sense on those sensitive to their plight. However, were this to settle into an enveloping melancholy, it would create a negative climate that could in turn immobilize efforts at rescue. In a melancholy spirit, one's strength abates. Also, to be rescued into a melancholy world is of questionable worth. Only with an affirmative, optimistic attitude to life in this world can we be effective advocates on behalf of those enduring oppression. It is a schizoid formula; but, on balance, the only viable alternative.

Massive denial breeds passivity, inaction, and resignation. It is the wrong response.

Rabbi Israel put a positive face on the matter: One who is full of joy is full of love for one's fellow creatures.

2

The Pursuit of Health

The Health Imperative

To be happy, to experience and enjoy the pleasures and delights of life, can be a narcissistic exercise. But it can also be a faith affirmation in the noblest sense, if the pleasures and delights are not ends in themselves, and instead are means toward a more meaningful end.

The experience of pleasure may be nothing more than self-indulgence, or nothing less than self-transcendence. Usually, it is a mixture of both. For example, the pleasure that one may experience while attending the wedding of a friend includes the pleasures of the palate, the good food and drink that are the norm for weddings. At the same time, there is a self-transcending pleasure, the feeling of being happy for others, of even making others happier through good wishes, kind remarks, lively dancing, and the bestowal of gifts.

We appreciate God's world better, and thus better appreciate God, through being open to absorbing the delights of the world in an optimistic, joyous spirit.[1] In this spirit, we are better able to enhance God's world by spreading optimism and joy to others.

Openness to the world and the ability to appreciate the world in all its grandeur are in large measure related to the nature of one's being. By "nature of one's being," we refer at once to state of mind and soundness of body. A melancholy or depressed state closes one off from the world; a healthy, contented state of mind opens one up to it.[2]

Soundness of body, a healthful, vigorous, energetic bodily state, also conduces to enjoyment of life's bounty. However, unlike the psychological state, or mental attitude, which is a powerful factor in determining how one approaches the world, the bodily state, while important, is not as powerful. Specifically, one may be weak, ill, or not well physically, and yet can enjoy life. Still, enjoyment of life is usually better achieved in a state of sound health.

Of course, it would be little less than absurd to suggest that we need to be healthy just so that we can more fully experience pleasure. Yet it is not off the mark to suggest that we are obliged to preserve our well-being in order that we can live longer and better. We affirm life by resolving to preserve the life with which we have been entrusted. We express faith, in the ultimate sense, when we protect the gift of life that has been granted to us by God and at the same time are thus better equipped, quantitatively and qualitatively, to appreciate the bounty of this world presented to us by God for our benefit.

It is thus more than apropos, in this discourse on pleasure, to focus on the obligations related to self-preservation that are basic to Judaism.

"Be exceedingly heedful of your selves. . . ."[3] This phrase of a verse in the Torah (literally teaching, or law, but referring here to the Bible, the Five Books of Moses), is the "elastic clause" which extends the obligation of self-preservation to all contingencies that may affect one's well-being.

The language of the passage is almost as instructive as its essential message. We are asked not merely to be heedful; we are asked to be "exceedingly heedful" of ourselves. This terminology (*me'od*) is rarely employed in the Torah. Its use here projects how important is the concept of self-preservation in Judaic theology. Other commandments we are obliged to observe; this commandment, the multifaceted commandment of self-preservation, we are obliged to observe in the extreme; steadfastly, vigilantly, uncompromisingly.

MODERN APPLICATION

The self-preservation obligation is obviously and understandably couched in general terms. The Torah does not give precise parameters or specific applications of this command, since health-related imperatives may vary from place to place and from generation to generation. For example, the diet of those living in warmer climates differs from the recommended diet for those living in colder ones.

Cigarette smoking is a prime example of a health-related imperative that changes from generation to generation. In previous generations, the question was whether one may smoke on a festival, whether smoking involved any contravention of Jewish law (halakhah).[4] The prevailing view was that if one respected the prohibitions entailed in kindling or extinguishing a fire, then smoking was allowed since the pleasure of smoking promoted relaxation, a legitimate enhancement of the festival spirit.

However, more recent research has revealed how cigarette smoking is a hazard to health; not only of the smoker, but of the bystanders who inhale secondhand smoke.[5] The question today is not whether one may smoke on the festivals, but at any time. And the answer coming forth from responsible Jewish religious authorities is that cigarette smoking contravenes the imperative to "Be exceedingly heedful of your selves." Cigarette smoking is injurious to health, and is condemned as a deadly poison which is forbidden by Jewish law, more forbidden than pork.

Of course, we have not yet fully digested the relatively newfound revelations concerning smoking, which make smoking tantamount to a suicidal act, albeit suicide on the installment plan. There are still pockets of resistance, those who claim that since cigarette smoking is a well-entrenched habit, God will surely protect us simpletons from the consequences of tar and nicotine.[6] In time, and one hopes before long, the realities of the dangers of smoking will themselves become entrenched, and will displace the tolerant attitudes some still maintain.

Then, the statement that smoking, according to Jewish law, is worse than eating pork, will not come as a shock. We judge the severity of a prohibition by the penalty suffered for its breach. The penalty, presently theoretical, for eating pork, is flagellation, 39 whips or less depending on one's level of tolerance,[7] administered by the Rabbinical

Court. Cigarette smoking, on the other hand, is a suicidal act, a murder of the self, which technically cannot be punished. The penalty can be imposed only after the breach;[8] with the suicide, it is then too late. One may argue about whether the delayed-action effects of smoking make smoking less liable to any penalty. The most relevant point is that cigarette smoking is in the general category of capital crime, not mere prohibition, as is the case with pork.

To a certain extent, the actual prescription for health preservation is fluid and fluctuates according to the place and time.[9] However, the Talmud, in statements dispersed over the breadth of Talmudic literature, provides profound insight into the many aspects of self-preservation as a major concern of Judaism.

Avoiding Danger

Consistent with the smoking/pork analogy, a prevailing theme in the Talmud is that anything dangerous demands greater scrupulousness than that which is merely prohibited.[10] A classic example of this principle is the case of mixture of various types. For example, should the fat from an animal that is not kosher (fit to be eaten, according to Jewish law), such as a horse or a tiger, fall into an urn full of fat that is kosher, that mixture is prohibited unless the ratio of kosher to nonkosher is at least 60 to 1. If there is 60 times as much kosher as nonkosher, the nonkosher contribution to the mixture is considered neutralized, and one may eat from the mixture.

However, if lethal poison should fall into a mixture, then even a 1,000 to 1 ratio will not neutralize the poison. In other words, even the slightest drop of poison that falls into the largest, otherwise edible mixture, renders the new concoction forbidden. Scrupulousness relative to health dangers is again projected as a religious value, forming an important component of Jewish ritual law.

The corollary to the prohibitive aspect, in which actions or habits detrimental to health are forbidden, is the positive fulfillment to take care of ourselves. "The soul that I (God) have placed in you, sustain it."[11] God asks those who have been blessed with life to nourish that life. God starts the process of life; the human being, through the care given to that life, plays a significant role in determining what the quantity and quality of that life will be.

On the verse, "And God will remove from you all sickness . . ,"[12] we find the following comment; "it is *from you* (in your power) that sickness should not befall you."[13] In another, more assertive comment, it is stated that God invokes heaven and earth as witnesses that premature death and pain come from excessive eating and drinking, and too much good times. Embarrassment, deteriorating eyesight early in life, and several diseases are all functions of human behavior, and directly related to undesirable behavior patterns.[14]

Failing health in its many forms results from abuse, be it of food and drink, or be it sexual promiscuity. The suggestion, not so subtle, is that the moral imperatives of the Torah have both spiritual and physiological implications. God calls heaven and earth as witnesses that nature which is respected is maintained and enhanced. Nature which is abused is harmed, even destroyed. This is the fundamental principle of human and environmental ecology. Earth not carefully fertilized and judiciously nourished will eventually cease to yield of its bounty. Polluted heavens will release acid rain. When heaven and earth do not function properly, they testify to human abuse of heaven and earth. When heaven and earth bestow of their resources, they testify to human care.[15]

This rule applies equally to the human body. Properly cared for, the human body will function as would be expected of a Godly creation. If the body is abused, its godliness denied, it will break down prematurely.

Conditional Destiny

No one lives forever, and the finality that is death eventually catches up with everyone. Those who respect the delicacy of their finiteness and sustain the God-given breath of life through a life of moderation, control, and care, are likely to live out their life span to the preordained limit. Those who ungratefully grab the gift of life and run to overindulgence are likely to race to premature death.

Thus, when Alexander the Great asked the sages of the south, "What should a person do in order to live?" they replied: "He should kill his *self* (penchant for overindulgence)." To the question, "What should a person do in order to die?" these sages replied, "He should overindulge himself."[16]

The Talmud observes that were a person to sell his *self* to a cannibal, he would demand a steep price, but through neglect of the self one sells one's own self for a very cheap price.[17]

Indeed, in the view of the Rabbis, of every 100 premature deaths, one may be an act of God, with the other 99 caused by sinful neglect of one's self.[18] This observation is applied even to Talmudic scholars, who die prematurely not because they are promiscuous and not because they steal, but because they are derelict in caring for their health.[19] This is a statement of fact; a lamentable fact, not an excuse.

The few Rabbinic comments presented here suggest a less than absolute concept of destiny. Each human being is destined to live a certain length of time. Thankfully, no one knows from the outset the duration of his or her life. Instead, we are obliged to live every day as if it were our last, as if that day's activity forms the lasting imprint to be placed on individual life.[20]

Additionally, our destiny of years, how many years have been granted, does not come with a guarantee. We reach the limit if we play by the rules, but forfeit the claim on any preordained destiny if life is abused. Destiny is therefore not absolute, it is conditional. It is hardly fair to expect that no matter what we do, the length of our days, in quantity and quality, will be the same. If we subject ourselves to abuse, and are neglectful of ourselves, we cannot expect that God will care as much about us. Relationship to God, as to humans, is a two-way dialogue. The Talmud suggests that the rules of nature implanted at creation contain the basic formulae that manifest the cause-effect destiny.

With regard to this cause-effect destiny, one may question why an obviously obese individual lives to the age of sixty or more, and why one who cares well for the self, watches the diet and exercises regularly, dies in the midforties. This question is based on the assumption that we are allotted the same number of years. With this assumption, it is difficult to explain why one who has abused the body should live longer than one who gave it scrupulous care.

In reality, however, the assumption that everyone is apportioned the same life span is erroneous. We do not know why,[21] but the life span destiny varies from person to person. The obese individual who lives to sixty may have been destined to live to eighty. The vigorous, healthy, careful individual who dies at the age of forty may have been destined to live only to thirty. We do not know, and are better off for it. We cannot know, for we then enter into a domain that belongs exclusively to God.

With "holy insecurity," and with concomitant assurance that the care we give to our own selves will enhance the quantity and quality of life, we resolve to do our best in all the dimensions of life; we leave the rest, including all the unanswerable questions, to God.

SOME RULES

All the rules for self-preservation as gleaned from the Torah and Talmud would yield a book of its own, encyclopedic in size. The general observations that follow, concerning a few crucial areas of human life, will provide sufficient insight into the breadth and depth of the Judaic concern for health.

One of the more important areas is the matter of diet: what we eat, when, how much, among other considerations.

The Talmud states that the bread of the morning, or a substantial breakfast, is good for the entire body.[22] Eating without drinking is considered dangerous, and can lead to the onset of intestinal diseases.[23] Here too a distinction is made, between a breakfast meal and a supper meal. In a breakfast meal, the failure to combine substantial liquids with the solid food intake is considered to be a health hazard.[24] This is so because breakfast is the meal that fuels the body, the body being in need of liquid for sustaining itself and avoiding dehydration over the course of a day's activity.

On the other hand, at a supper meal, which would normally come prior to but not immediately before going to sleep, there is advantage in having liquids together with a solid, but this is more to help in the digestive process of the food than because of the dangers involved in possible dehydration.[25] However, it should be noted that the need to digest food properly is in itself vital for the health of the human body.

One who eats and stands up immediately, or drinks and stands up immediately, is judged to be closer to death than to life,[26] ostensibly because by getting up immediately after the eating, one leaves little time for the food to settle and to digest.

With regard to the choice of food, those who eat a food that does not agree with their own systems, that is disliked and possibly deleterious to one's health, transgress against three basic principles. Such persons have acted shamefully towards the self, have acted shamefully towards the food, and additionally have recited a blessing that is not proper.[27]

These three transgressions are a telling statement about the care one must exercise in approaching the choice of food. By eating food that does not agree with one's system, one has shown a lack of caring, and has even acted with disrespect towards one's own body; this is considered sinful. Additionally, the food itself, since it has not achieved its purpose of enhancing the human body, has been shamed and desecrated. Food was put on this earth to enhance our health and welfare, and it is our obligation to put that food to such use. When we abuse ourselves, we also perforce abuse the food, and therefore detract from the sacred purpose for which food was placed on this earth. Finally, any blessing over food that is so abused is in itself sinful, since we are hereby blessing God and thanking God and then descrating that to which we ascribe a blessing. Reciting God's name and associating it with such an abominable behavior is a desecration of God's name.

HYGIENE

Additionally, the Talmud speaks of a prohibition against drinking from exposed waters if there is a present danger that there may be substances in the water that would adversely affect one's health.[28] Translating this into the modern idiom would imply a prohibition against drinking from any water or eating any food if there is reason to suspect that such drink or food may be germ infested and likely to transmit disease.

In former days, there was a custom to wash one's hands following the conclusion of a meal and before the recitation of the grace after meals. This was done in order to cleanse the hands from certain poisonous salts that could possibly cause blindness if one placed the salted fingers in one's eye.[29] Many still maintain this custom, even though the presence of such poisonous salts is not a threatening reality in contemporary times.[30] The washing of the hands remains as a reminder of the need to maintain a modicum of cleanliness not only during the meal, but also after it, and in our regular activities. Such cleanliness will avert the problems associated with unhygienic practices.

Of singular importance in the matter of diet is the question of amounts. More die from overeating than from undereating, or in the Talmudic parlance, more people are killed by the pot than are bloated by famine.[31] The rich person is the one who has the privy right next to the table.[32] In previous generations, a privy was a luxury that only the wealthy could have in such close proximity. However, another interpretation is that the spiritually wealthy person is the one who keeps the privy in mind when eating. Such a person always is aware that excess eventually leaves the body, and becomes waste. Rather than wasting one's money on eating that which serves no purpose, the spiritually wealthy person measures what is eaten and digests only that which is necessary.[33]

The Talmud suggests a very definite procedure for clearing out one's body before one eats. It is considered wrong to eat before one has cleared out one's system from the residue of previous meals.[34] The Talmud recommends walking-stopping, walking-stopping, walking-stopping, perhaps to get the system working, then cleansing one's self, and only afterwards sitting down to eat.[35] It is advisable that one take one's time in the privy, to allow for a most thorough cleansing.[36] Those who suffer from the inability to thoroughly cleanse, are urged to stand up and sit down repeatedly to counteract the constipation.[37] Another suggestion is a left-right movement to and fro.[38] Others say that maybe the best remedy is to focus one's attention and concentrate on the process of cleansing, and not think of other things that might serve to impede the process.[39]

The matter of cleansing one's self of one's bodily excess is an issue of serious importance in Judaic religious law. One who "holds the self in," and delays the release of excess that is ready to leave the system, transgresses the prohibitive command, "You shall not abominate yourselves."[40] The Talmud hereby establishes that proper bodily hygiene is in fact a biblical imperative and not just simply good advice.

One of the best ways to avoid intestinal difficulties is to cleanse out the system when the body signals the readiness for such cleansing.[41] A Talmudic scholar is not allowed to live in a city which does not have proper privy facilities for the cleansing of one's body.[42] Although normally it is advisable not to think too highly of one's self, in this respect one is allowed to see one's self as a scholar,[43] because the need that is hereby addressed is one that applies to everyone. Obviously, a scholar, through individual behavior, sets the tone and provides the lead example for the population, and therefore has a greater responsibility to seek out the proper facilities; but the obligation to set up the proper logistics for taking care of one's internal hygiene applies to everyone.

RESTING AND WORKING

There is obviously more to bodily health and vigor than the matter of eating, drinking, and sifting out the excess and eliminating it from the body. There is the state of contentment, the rest and relaxation that the human body needs, among other things, to maintain freshness and vitality. The human being needs a certain amount of sleep, not too little and not too much. It is suggested that the proper daily amount of sleep is 8 hours, or one third of the day.[44] The right amount is healthful for the system, whereas too much sleep is not beneficial and is in fact harmful to the system. One needs to maintain a delicate balance between activity and relaxation; too much relaxation, or too much sleep, can possibly cause a harmful atrophy.[45]

Additionally, the states of sleep and activity are almost polar opposites, and it is not advisable to jump from sleep into activity without gradual acclimatization. The Talmud considers among those who are closer to death than to life, one who gets up suddenly from sleep and immediately launches into activity.[46] One needs to maintain a sense of balance not only in the amount of time allotted for sleep, but also in terms of how one eases from the state of slumber into the state of activity.

The balance that is most desirable in sleep is also most vital with regard to exercise. Bodily vigor is essential; in the words of the Talmud, a life infused with bodily vigor is the best of all blessings.[47] Judaism looks very favorably upon the "work ethic" not only because it is better to be self-supporting than to be a drain on society,[48] but because the sweat from working is healthful to the bodily system.[49] Additionally, the sweat from sitting in a sauna is considered of a very beneficial nature to the human body.[50]

Even the sweat of a sick person is considered a good sign—a sign that the fever has broken and that the body is on the way to regaining its equilibrium.

Here too a balance must be maintained, and overexertion is ill advised.[51] Lifting up weights beyond one's capacity is quite harmful and actually may sap the strength of an individual rather than give that person strength. Exercise that continually but methodically raises the power potential of the individual is quite all right, but a sudden jump into a weight category that is beyond present capacity is extremely dangerous.

Balance in one's habits also applies to the psychological dimension. Specifically, a balanced form of behavior that does not allow for the extreme form of expression, namely angry outbursts, is strongly recommended.[52] The Talmud views the calmness and equanimity that one maintains with one's own family, and also extends to society in general, as conducive to longevity.[53] Envy, greed, lust, all imbalanced and distorted forms of expression, drive the person out of the world prematurely.[54] Sighing, invoking a tone of resignation, complaint, or bitterness, is seen as a type of expression that can harm the individual.[55]

Good behavioral habits, including a sense of acceptance of others, tolerance toward individuals and situations that might possibly be anger evoking, the capacity to take life in stride and not be overwhelmed by a crisis, are all vital for maintaining a healthful balance and viable perspective; to perhaps express in thought and in deed an optimism, an affirmative approach to life that reinforces physical health with spiritual vitality.

BREATH OF LIFE

We are obligated to be grateful for the life that has been granted to us, literally to bless God for every breath of life that we are able to breathe.[56] Primarily, this attitude enables us to take in stride the difficulties that may confront us and possibly depress or overwhelm us. Before attacking any problem, it is necessary to feel the gratitude for having the life to be able to tackle the problem and thus, in this balanced approach, to avoid the psychological problems and traumas that arise from a thankless approach to life.

To be able to thank God for every breath, it is obviously useful that the air we inhale be fresh and clean. The Talmud relates of a student of Rabbi Akiva (second century sage), that he fell ill, and when Rabbi Akiva came to visit him, the student, out of respect, cleaned up the house. Because of this the air that he breathed was cleaner and through this he was restored to health.[57] Even in Talmudic times there was an awareness of the importance of clean air and its affect on one's health.

This point is driven home in the regulation that the furnaces that burned materials had to be at least 50 cubits (approximately 75 feet) from the city limits.[58] There was an awareness that the pollution emitted from flames can be harmful to those inhaling that air. This clean air regulation has particular relevance for modern society, with all the pollutants emitted from cigarettes, automobiles, and factories. If we are to be grateful to God for the air that we breathe, it stands to reason that we should be breathing God's air, and not air contaminated with distinctly human contributions.

PREVENTION

The best medicine, in almost all circumstances, is preventive medicine. We are best advised to value and honor the commands of the physician before needing that physician.[59]

What applies to the eyes applies to the entire body. Regarding the eyes, it is cautioned that sight does not fail the human being except by bad habit, the carelessness which, through failure to preserve sight, threatens its loss.[60] Carelessness in general can lead to the loss of one's health and the onset of illness.

A balance in life, an avoidance of any extreme, is perhaps the best general approach. An eloquent statement in this regard is that one should not sit too much for that may cause piles, one should not stand too much for that may be harmful to the heart, and one should not walk too much for that may be harmful to the eyes. Instead, one should balance between these three, and spend one third of one's time sitting, one third standing and one third walking.[61]

Balance, discipline, control, perspective—these are the key words for physical and spiritual well-being. This does not mean that the presence of this balance guarantees freedom from illness. It does, however, show that one cares about one's well-being, and is a testimony to God that one appreciates the life that God has given. As a believing people, we are sure that God takes notice of this; our concern for and our nurturing of life is taken into the ultimate equation for how one's life will unfold. The outcome may not always meet our wishes, nor will it obviate all theological problems. However, before we venture to raise theological questions, we must be sure that we are on solid ground: the solid ground of having taken meticulous care of that precious gift of life that has been entrusted to us.

3

Avoiding Pain

Defining Pain

In the pursuit of health, in maintaining a sound physical state, we are provided with a usually accurate indicator of activities or habits that should be avoided. Abuse of health is usually followed, sooner or later, by pain, the pain of a limb, organ, or body not adequately cared for, even ignored. This is not to suggest that those who meticulously guard their health will avoid pain; but those who neglect their health are generally more likely to experience pain.

In spite of the connection between health and pain, the matter of avoiding pain is fundamentally an independent issue, independent of whether it affects health. The question that needs to be confronted is— may one subject oneself to pain, and if so, under what circumstances?

Essentially, Judaism takes a dim view of subjecting the self to unnecessary pain.[1] We are here to enjoy God's world, to experience its grandeur and majesty. In pain, we hurt and suffer, and are repelled from the world. The masochist, who enjoys pain, is the exception, an aberration from the norm, whose criteria deviate from what is healthful and desirable.

In addressing the issue of pain, it is difficult, yet vital, to define as precisely as possible what is considered pain. The fitness buff who stretches the body's muscles to the limit undoubtedly experiences pain. The homemaker who rushes to put the house in order may feel some pain in the strain to get the job done. The individual who flies long distances will usually feel some pain as the cabin pressure changes. Obviously, these activities, though they may involve pain, are not intended for the pain, nor is the pain a form of denial.

Actually, we are asked to like working, and to detest acting as a superior.[2] Work may involve strain, and giving orders may be less taxing physically, yet work is praised and giving orders disparaged. There are obvious moral components to this dialectic, in that one is better off "doing," being involved in the nitty-gritty. Giving orders is a detached and aloof form of behavior, demeaning to others, that hardly conduces to human sensitivity. On the other hand, the sweat of work is considered to be good for the body.[3]

It seems that growth- or health-oriented pain is considered a positive feature of human life. Balance is necessary, as it is in so many other areas of human experiences. Work is one of those activities which in excess is harmful, but in moderation is beneficial.[4] Intensive work saps the person's strength.[5] On the other hand, idleness leads to atrophy.[6] One who has no work should, if there is a courtyard in shambles or a field in desolation, occupy the self with that courtyard or field.[7] In other words, work is so important that if there is no work, one must seek it out, or create it.

POSITIVE PAIN

With no strain, with no stress, one is spiritually dead. Being immersed in life brings with it inevitable strains and stresses, but these are growth- and health-oriented realities easily incorporated into a meaningful life affirmation.

There are pains that may impose themselves on the human being in the course of normal activity, pain that is more in the form of discomfort. The pain in the ears during cabin pressure change in flight, the pain of being compressed into a crowded bus or train and occasionally being stepped on, being fastened tightly in place with a seat-belt, are all normal, run-of-the-mill, mild inconveniences that are almost impossible to avoid. Were we to try to avoid all such discomfort, we would be bound by a life-style characterized by obsessive anxiety to avoid all restrictions that impinge on one's comfort.

Success in such an endeavor, were it even attainable, would render us incapable of appreciating complete ease, since we would not have any of the mildly disconcerting experiences that then enable us fully to appreciate comfort.[8] As part of a syndrome, such avoidance obsession may also eventually render us insensitive to others and their own pain, surely not an ideal way to live.

The inability to experience pain is a deficit situation in more than one way. A person who suffers from a nerve malfunction through which sensation is lost may avoid pain, but suffer severe damage because the pain alarm does not send a danger signal. Such a person may get burned and not feel it, or be severely cut without realizing it, until much harm is done. Pain is often a warning that alerts the person to a potentially harmful situation. A headache may indicate that one is abusing the body, working too long hours, not gaining enough sleep. Pain in the chest may indicate something functionally wrong. The human being whose body gives off warning signals before potentially tragic situations, and who is alert to these signals, is protected.

That pernicious disease, cancer, would be much less a threat if there were clear signals from the body. There are some symptoms, such as a prolonged cold, or a lesion that does not heal, that arouse suspicion and indicate that a medical checkup is appropriate. But we would all be better off if there were some identifiable sensation, even a sharp pain, that gave us advance warning, and a chance to detect cancer in its early stages.

Another area where inability to experience pain manifests itself adversely is in the world of emotions. *Melancholia anaesthetica* is the term that describes the condition in which the individual cannot mourn or cry, properly express grief, or feel sadness or the pain of loss. One can literally become melancholy over anesthetized emotion. There is hardly a greater despair than that of those who despair because they are unable to be sad.[9] It turns out that the ability to experience pain and loss is fundamental to the human being and basic to life itself.

Pain and Commandment

Even though the ability to experience pain, loss, and suffering is crucial to life, and to the appreciation of health, contentment, and love, there are *no* direct prescriptions within the Judaic legal code that are obligations to experience pain. It may well be that there are times when the actualization of a command, or the adherence to a prohibition, may involve pain, but the experience of the pain is never the direct focus of the command.

One may conjecture that it matters little whether the pain is experienced as a direct commandment or as a result of being commanded, but philosophically, and in terms of general approach to life, the difference is quite significant. The fact that there are no commandments to experience pain is, effectively, a definitive statement. It is a statement that the experience of pain in and of itself is not a commandment, and is more likely than not a detraction from life and from the affirmation of God. The fact that there are some commandments that may tangentially involve pain is an accident that is not necessarily unavoidable. Commandments may bring, in certain circumstances and for certain individuals, the experience of pain; but that is not the intent of the observance, nor is it a necessary quality of the observance.

Fasting

For example, there is an obligation to fast on the Day of Atonement.[10] This is the only biblically ordained fast. There are other fasts in the Jewish calendar, but they are rabbinic in origin, including the Fast of Gedaliah, the Fast of Esther, the Fast of the 10th of Tevet, the Fast of the 17th of Tamuz, and the Fast of the 9th of Av.[11] The Day of Atonement remains not merely the sole biblically ordained fast day; it is also the only fast day not associated with mournful or even cataclysmic events in Jewish history. As a matter of fact, tradition appropriates to Yom Kippur a sense of forgiveness and joy, historically linked to the atonement extended to the Israelites after the Golden Calf episode; atonement which manifested itself in the transmission of a new set of tablets which were handed down on Yom Kippur, the Day of Atonement.[12] The Talmud later reports that Yom Kippur was a very celebrative day in the Jewish calendar.[13]

Yet Yom Kippur, the Day of Atonement, is a day of total abstinence. From before sundown just prior to the Day of Atonement, until nighttime on the Day of Atonement, a period usually lasting close to 26 hours, no eating, drinking, washing, oiling of the skin, or wearing of leather shoes is permitted.[14] In addition, marital relations are also proscribed.[15] On the Day of Atonement, which is referred to in the Bible as a Sabbath,[16] all the work restrictions in force on the Sabbath are likewise operative.[17]

Fasting of course can be a painful experience for many. Being deprived of food and drink for a lengthy period of time can cause headaches, faintness, possible dehydration, and other assorted problems. Yet the fulfillment of the letter and the spirit of Yom Kippur, the Day of Atonement, is totally divorced from the notion of pain.

Those who assume that merely by subjecting themselves to pain and sacrifice for one entire day they are thereby fulfilling the wishes of God, are making a serious mistake.[18] On the other hand, those who think that they have compromised the meaning of Yom Kippur because they went through the entire day without feeling hungry are also mistaken.

Yom Kippur is a day of total, uncompromising meditation. It is a day when the human being is divorced from material concerns of all dimensions, including work creativity, even eating and drinking. It is a day when the human being is literally forced, by virtue of the hedge of legislation surrounding the day, to focus inward, to examine the nature of his deeds over the course of the past year, to repent of all wrong that had been committed, and to express regret over all worthy actions that could have been taken but were not.[19] Yom Kippur likewise involves resolve for the future, to correct the wrongs of the past, to redress situations that call for compensation, and to embark on a life qualitatively superior as a result of the atonement experience.[20]

The biblical prescription for Yom Kippur indicates that such total mediation cannot be achieved when one is involved in the material world. Therefore a total detachment from the material world is prescribed. It is quite likely that an individual who is wholly thrown into this meditative spirit will be oblivious to his own physical condition, and may not even be aware of the hunger and the thirst that would normally plague one deprived of sustenance for so long. When one transcends the self into the dimension of meditation, the physical concerns may effectively retreat into the background.

On the other hand, individuals who celebrate the Day of Atonement as an exercise in clock-watching, looking at the time to see how much longer they must endure the agony of fasting, but achieving nothing in the realm of serious meditation, may have experienced real pain, but they have not truly experienced the Day of Atonement.

The observance of Yom Kippur thus is an instructive model for the Judaic notion of pain. It is probably the command that comes closest to legislating the experience of pain. Yet, upon analysis, Yom Kippur is shown to be an observance which, though it might tangentially involve pain, is certainly neither philosophically nor causally directly linked to the experience of pain.

CIRCUMCISION

Another commandment ostensibly associated with pain is the obligation to circumcise the child at the ripe age of 8 days.[21] Circumcision is a very significant experience: the entry of the child into a covenantal relationship with God. That covenant is imprinted on the very organ that generates posterity. It is a covenant that is transgenerational.

Circumcision itself, although it involves only the removal of a foreskin, is undoubtedly painful. Nevertheless, here too the pain is not the essential component of the procedure. Witness the fact that a boy who is born without a foreskin, literally born circumcised, need not go through a painful procedure in order to effect the covenantal pact. A relatively simple and painless procedure is prescribed for such a contingency.[22]

Also, since the circumcision procedure takes place at the age of only 8 days,[23] it may be conjectured, though with obvious limitations, that circumcision at such an early stage is much less painful than later on, when the child's nerve-endings are more developed. In most circumcisions, the child cries for a moment or two, and almost immediately returns to normal. With an older male, the likelihood is that the pain would be felt more intensely, and for a much longer period of time.

As a matter of fact, precisely because of the sensitivity to even this minor degree of pain for the child, the blessing that is normally recited at happy events, *sheheheyanu* (Blessed are you, God, who has given us life and sustained us, and enabled us to celebrate this time), is omitted at the circumcision ceremony, in deference to the young child for whom this experience involves some pain.[24] It is as if we are told that we have no right to rejoice excessively, even though this is a significant moment, if it is at the expense of someone else's pain.

In the traditional circumcision ceremonial, the baby is actually held in the hands of a person called the *sandek,* who is honored with this privilege.[25] This is significant not only ritually, but also because of the psychological implications. Were the child to be fastened on a circumstraint (a specially designed device that ties the child down), as is sometimes the case, the child not only is subjected to a painful experience, but at the same time is detached from tactile contact. Often the child will cry more when the legs are bound in on the circumstraint than it will during the circumcision itself. The fact that the child is held during the circumcision gives the child the feeling of connectedness to humans, which is so vital.

Experiments have shown that dogs, for example tend to have an increased heartbeat if they are administered shocks. However, if the dogs are petted during the administering of the shocks, the heartbeat does not accelerate, and in certain situations and under certain conditions, may actually slow down.[26] This is an indication of how vital and helpful human touch can be to a person who is going through a painful experience.

All of this serves to project how sensitive Judaism is to pain, and how it seeks to neutralize the pain as much as possible. Again, it should be emphasized that the circumcision itself does not require the experience of pain. For those fortunate enough not to experience pain during the act of circumcision, so much the better.

PROCREATION AND LABOR PAINS

Another interesting instance of a pain-associated commandment is the first commandment of the Bible, "Be fruitful and multiply."[27] Actually, the fulfillment of procreation starts off with an intensely pleasurable experience, the sexual union. However, 9 months later or thereabouts, there is excruciating pain experienced by the woman—the pain of childbirth.

Childbirth is an instance when the experience of pain is not disassociated from the commandment. After the experience of the Garden, Eve and, in fact, women in general, are told that they will give birth in agony.[28] This does not mean that a woman who is capable of avoiding the pain through acupuncture, hypnosis, or even anesthetic, transgresses when so doing.[29] The statement relates more to a fact of life and, like all facts of life, is always subject to variation depending on the circumstances, and the individual involved.

However, whereas in the instance of the Day of Atonement, or of circumcision, the pain is incidental to the fulfillment, and certainly philosophically disjointed from it, in childbirth the pain is actually linked by the biblical verse, "in renunciation shall you bear children."[30] This is problematic and at the same time also ironic. Concerning the procreation commandment, unlike fasting or circumcision, the act which leads to impregnation—sexual relations—is probably the ultimate of pleasures.

In strict legal terms, the commandment to "be fruitful and multiply" is the actual obligation. In this sense the sexual act is the precursor, the necessary action which makes procreation possible. In other words, whereas with regard to the Day of Atonement and circumcision the *pain* is incidental to the fulfillment, with regard to procreation the *pleasure* is incidental to the fulfillment.

This leaves us with a simple, yet crucial question. How do we come to grips with the procreation commandment insofar as it affects the concept of pain in Judaic thinking?

An interesting anomaly concerning the procreation commandment is the fact that the obligation and the fulfillment are directed at the male of the species. It is the man who is obliged to "be fruitful" and to "multiply,"[31] and it is thus the man who fulfills the commandment when having children.[32] The woman is not commanded to be fruitful and multiply, and when she gives birth, she does not fulfill the commandment, since she is not obligated in that commandment in the first place.[33]

It seems odd, and even unfair, that the woman, who is carrying the child within her for 9 months, at great sacrifice to her own life because of all the risks involved in pregnancy, and all the discomforts, physical and emotional, should not even be given the "credit" for having persevered through such trying circumstances. However, once our appreciation of the Judaic concept of pain is inserted into this procreation equation, the matter is clarified.

Giving birth is painful, both during intense labor and in the actual birth process itself, and even for a significant period after birth. Were the woman obligated to have children, it would be an instance of legislated pain. It would be a biblically ordained imperative to undergo pain, unavoidable pain in most instances, for the purpose of fulfilling a commandment.[34]

As has been pointed out, with other precedents, namely fasting and circumcision, the pain involved is incidental and philosophically independent of the fulfillment. With childbirth, one cannot dodge the matter of pain related to the commandment as easily. The Bible directs the obligation to have children to the male of the species, who does not go through intense labor, does not have the actual pain associated with childbirth, and is linked to the process only through the pleasure component at the very onset of the impregnation process. The woman has no obligation to have children, because she cannot be obligated to suffer pain.

Painless Commands

In other words, the marital dynamics that are created by this commandment are quite unique. The man is obligated to have children; the woman, because having children involves such intense pain, is under no pressure, from the biblical perspective, to have children. If she decides that she wants children, then it is her own decision, entered into at her own initiative, with obvious encouragement from tradition, from her own parental model, and from religious teachings.

The man, who may want children, and whether he wants them or not is obligated to have them, is thus obliged to seek out, for marriage, a woman who shares with him this desire to have children. If he does not succeed in finding such a woman, then he obviously will not be able to fulfill the commandment.

But that cannot be held against him, for there are countless commandments that individuals may be unable to perform because of circumstance. A person who is penniless obviously cannot give anything to charity,[35] a man who is impotent cannot physically have children,[36] a hemophiliac may not survive a circumcision and hence is not allowed to place his life in jeopardy.[37] These are instances, among many others, in which the fulfillment of the commandment is rendered impossible by virtue of circumstance. This same understanding would apply to a man who tries to find a woman to marry, but is unable to find a suitable partner.

The paradigm offered in this commandment to "be fruitful and multiply" is instructive. It establishes balance in the marital union, in that the husband-wife relationship is not one of a demand quality, but one of agreement to common principles without the coercion of biblical command. It is so structured that the one who actually goes through the pain component of the procreation fulfillment is not obliged to fulfill that commandment, while the one for whom the procreation procedure is pleasurable only is indeed obligated.

Translated into the marital context, it states in very prosaic terms that man should never burden his wife with obligations that God did not impose upon the woman. The woman goes through intense pain for the sake of fulfillment, and that should be appreciated as a free-willed, spontaneous act of immense meaning and significance, rather than as an act that results from coercion.

In a word, the woman is not obligated to be fruitful and multiply, for this would legislate that she must go through pain. Compulsory procreation would, in effect, be an obligation to experience pain. This runs contrary to the Judaic ethos, which gives to pain no religious value per se. The first commandment, to be fruitful and multiply, in its chronology as the first command, addresses the primary act which regenerates and replenishes humankind; it also makes a very pointed statement about pleasure and pain. Through its exempting women from the commandment and its obligating men only, the general framework for commandment as an affirmation, in joy, of life, is firmly entrenched from the very outset.

Approaches to Suffering

In Talmudic writings, one encounters various statements concerning suffering. Some take a dim view of suffering, and express the desire to avoid suffering. On the other hand, there are statements that speak positively and affirmatively about suffering. In the middle ground are many passages that speak about unavoidable suffering in accepting terms, taking the view that if the suffering persists, one should try to make the most of it, and use it as a vehicle for repentance and growth. An example of the first type of reaction to suffering—the desire not to be afflicted with suffering, is the prayer that sins be erased, but not through affliction.[38] Another is the statement that neither the suffering nor its reward is desired.[39]

Examples of the second attitude to suffering—the affirmative, positive approach, are evident in such statements as "suffering is precious."[40] The third approach—the positive value of suffering after the fact, taking the unavoidable suffering and using it as a vehicle for growth, is evident in such statements as "if a person sees that affliction is coming upon the self, the person should investigate his deeds."[41]

It is evident that affliction, the pain of suffering, has rehabilitative value. Pain acts as an alarm clock for people who may have behaved in a cavalier manner towards life, taking life with all its bounty for granted, and even abusing their responsibilities. Suffering stops the person in his tracks, and forces the person to rethink values and to reorder priorities.

There can be little question that a righteous life lived with sincerity and authenticity, and thus free of any affliction or suffering, is the ideal.[42] It is only when lack of authenticity, and deviation from righteousness, come into play, that affliction with its corrective potentialities is considered worthwhile. When affliction does come, the proper attitude to it is vital. One for whom the affliction actually rules over the body is in the category of a person whose life is not a life.[43] The accent here is on the idea that the suffering has "dominion" over the person, rather than the person having dominion over the suffering.

Herein one encounters the suggestion that suffering, when it comes, should elicit the type of reaction from the human being that is a growth response rather than a capitulation response. When it is a growth response, the person actually transmutes the suffering into an achievement, and in fact rules over the suffering, using it to full human spiritual advantage. When the suffering beats the person down, it is usually the result of a capitulation response; the individual has surrendered. That is the type of reaction that should be avoided.

PROPER ATTITUDE TOWARD SUFFERING

Ultimately, our full understanding of suffering is limited, as expressed in the Talmudic phraseology: "It is not within our capacity to explain the tranquillity of the wicked, and not even the affliction of the righteous."[44] Though suffering should be avoided if possible, if it comes unavoidably and inescapably, it is then futile to be wracked with philosophical questions. Instead, it is essential to surmount the situation through the proper attitude and approach to suffering.

Ironically, in taking the proper approach to the pain and the suffering, the actual physical component—the pain associated with the suffering—is often alleviated. The statement, "Whoever rejoices in the afflictions which are brought upon the self brings salvation to the world,"[45] is a broad, general statement that speaks volumes about the potential meaning in suffering. It is fair to assume that no individual escapes this world without some form of suffering.[46] The suffering may vary in intensity, but there are always disappointments, upsets, traumas, and possibly even tragedies. If everyone would react to a suffering type of situation, be it of a minor or more severe nature, with capitulation and resignation, the world would be doomed. Everyone would be burdened with melancholy and depression because of the suffering; useful, vital existence would become almost impossible.

Instead, one must approach life understanding that there will be afflictions, that there will be pain, that there will be upsets, but that the meaning of life is not compromised by such experiences. One must still be able to transcend these situations and approach life with optimism, even with joy. It is only through this approach that the world can maintain its vitality and viability.

Thus, whoever rejoices in the afflictions brought upon the self, which essentially means that whoever can remain happy in spite of the afflictions with which that person is burdened, brings salvation to the world: specifically by being an example of how, in spite of suffering, one is still able to hold one's head high, to wake up in the morning with gusto and resolve, and go through the day imbued with a sense of purpose.

It is related of the Hasidic Rabbi, Itche Mayer of Gur, that he lost 13 sons and yet was still able to go about his responsibilities with his customary zeal. When asked how he could reconcile his fate with his faith in God, and how he could find meaning in this suffering, he answered to the effect that no one who has gone through any suffering could complain about not wanting to go on in life, because one could always point to himself, Itche Mayer, as having lost so many sons yet still maintaining steadfast faith in God and involvement in life. If he could do it, then anyone else should be able to do it. This was, for Itche Mayer, the meaning of his suffering.

In the Judaic classic on suffering, Job reconnects to life when he is addressed by God. The reason for his suffering was not revealed, but in receiving communication from God, he realized there must be a meaning to the suffering, and to life.

This attitude is further embedded in Judaic consciousness through a practice that is normative in situations of joy and of sorrow. In both instances, one is obliged to recite a blessing.[47] For joyful situations, we bless God who is good and makes good things happen for others.[48] In situations of tragedy, we bless God who is "the True Judge."[49] The texts of the blessings are obviously different, since they address different situations. However, the contexts of the blessings are the same. In instances of both joy and sorrow, of pleasure and of pain, we affirm our belief, and express our commitment to life. In other words, no matter what the circumstances, we do not let either ecstacy or mourning derail individuals from the path of life.

A Problematic Statement

One statement, among others in the Talmud, seems to stand out as almost a recommendation that one seek out pain. It is the statement that the authentic Jewish way is to "eat bread with salt, to drink water in measure, to sleep on the ground, and live a life of pain."[50] Taken literally, this statement contradicts almost everything that has been stated previously in this volume. It indicates that pain is more than not undesirable; it is actually worth pursuing. It is identified as *the* authentic Jewish way.

However, if this statement is to be taken literally, then any individual who is blessed with plenty, who is able to eat more than just bread and water, and has a comfortable bed, is actually transgressing, or at least is not living in the authentic Jewish way. This is an obvious absurdity, and it has never been suggested that this is a normative theological proposition. One is therefore obliged to offer a more homiletic interpretation of this statement.

One possible explanation is that the statement refers not to a necessity, but to a contingency. It is *not necessary* to live in pain and in suffering, but in a situation where pain and suffering confront the individual, where these contingencies are unavoidable realities, the authentic Jewish way is to persevere even on bread and water, and sleeping on the floor.[51] In this view, the statement becomes another affirmation of the basic attitude to pain herein proposed; namely, that one should not seek out the pain, but if the pain seeks out the person, or the privation besets the person, the person should be able to surmount the circumstance and persevere through the difficult times.

Historically, it is difficult to deny the fact that adherence to this statement has stood the Jewish people in good stead. It is precisely the ability of previous generations to persevere through trying times that has allowed for a posterity, and for existent Jewish communities in contemporary times. Communal salvation has derived from the collective capacity to affirm life even in the most painful and tragic circumstances.

4

Countering Depression

NORMAL DEPRESSION

In expounding the theme of pleasure, it is common to think that the opposite of pleasure is pain. This is certainly true, but it does not preclude the existence of other antitheses. One of them is depression, or sadness. The person who experiences pleasure feels gratified, happy, affirmative, optimistic, joyous; the depressed person feels melancholy, downcast, forlorn, upset, among a host of other negative emotions.

It is possible for an individual simultaneously to experience pain and pleasure. For example, a parent who is suffering from the effects of a broken arm or leg, and is in excruciating pain, can still feel greatly pleased when a child is getting married, or when another family joy is being experienced. Certain types of pain do not preclude the experience of pleasure even in the throes of the pain. However, the person who is melancholy and depressed, overcome with sadness, has such a bleak outlook on life that even the pleasurable events are usually not experienced in their completeness, but are dismissed as temporary aberrations in an otherwise unhappy life.

Depression in its extreme form is a serious affliction. However, depression comes in all forms and in varying doses, and at one time or another probably afflicts the majority of the population.[1] Thankfully, most individuals are able to weather the depression storm, and come out of the melancholy mood, again able to confront life with all its potential.

It is, after all, normal that in certain circumstances one should feel melancholy and sad. A person who has suffered a great personal tragedy, such as the loss of a loved one, cannot help but be depressed. It is healthful to confront this depression directly, not to run away from it, or to pretend that life can go on normally without any mourning or sadness. Such an evasion of a natural response only delays the eventual confrontation with the mourning. This delayed grief reaction, coming from unresolved grief, can be more painful than the actual, on-the-spot experience of mourning itself.

At the same time that it is natural and desirable to confront a tragic situation honestly and forthrightly, be it the loss of a loved one, of a job, or of one's fortune, it is also vital that one does not become overwhelmed by the sorrow, and unable to extricate oneself from the depressed feeling. Life has its ups and downs; and we are asked to endure the downs, so that we can all the more fully experience the ups.

EXCEPTION TO THE RULE

In Jewish tradition, depression and the melancholy feeling are conceived to be the exception to the rule. That is to say, there are times, and legitimate situations, that evoke a melancholy mood, but as a rule, the feeling of optimism and affirmation of life should be the dominant theme. When the Talmud states that the Divine Presence does not manifest itself in a spirit of melancholy,[2] it is asserting that the basic Judaic life-style is actualized and affirmed in a spirit of optimism and joy rather than in a spirit of depression and sadness. How can one be expected to wake up in the morning with verve and confidence, and to thank God for being placed in the world,[3] when one would rather not be in the world, when one feels so sad and low and that one really has no sense of drive and purpose? Prayer too, says the Talmud, cannot be approached with a melancholy spirit.[4]

One may even go so far as to say that failing any biological factor that may be implicated in the depression, a philosophically based or attitudinally provoked depression is inconsistent with Jewish religious expression. In other words, a truly religious individual, in the profound understanding of the term, by definition cannot be depressed.

The Talmud speaks of some of the major behavior manifestations by which one can judge an individual's character. They are, in the Hebrew, *kees, kos,* and *kaas.*[5] This Hebrew alliteration is translated in the English as referring to one's charity habits (*kees*—one's pocket), one's drinking habits (*kos*—one's cup), and one's temperament, or tendency to become angry (*kaas*—anger). Others add a fourth character variable, namely one's laughter.[6] One can say that the individual capacity to laugh, be it at oneself or with others, to be a joyful participant and player on the world's stage, is also a gauge of one's character, and of the nature of one's philosophical outlook on life.

A depressed attitude to the world is usually combined with, if not rooted in, a negative feeling toward one's self. It is in this context that one can best understand what has been described as a great general principle of Judaism: "Love your neighbor as yourself."[7] In strict legal terms, this statement deals with respect for that which belongs to others. In other words, the more precise reading of this verse would be: "love that which accrues to your neighbor as if it were your own."[8] This translates as an obligation to be respectful of your friend's property, your friend's dignity, your friend's self-esteem, as if it were yours.

However, the actual sense of the verse imparts more than just a legalistic meaning. It speaks to the necessity for an individual to have a good appreciation of the self, if there is to be a good appreciation of others. In other words, we are asked to like others or love others, with that feeling of liking or love being anchored in a positive attitude towards the self.

It is immediately recognized that a person who is down on the self, who does not like his own self, can hardly be expected to like others. The person who does not like the self is usually sad and "low," and that very darkened view of the self is extended towards others. The biblical obligation to love others is therefore linked to the love of oneself. We are asked, at once, to love ourselves, to have an appreciation of ourselves and our capacities, and thus to extend that same appreciation to others. No more nor less is expected of us than to put all of humanity into the same affirmative approach, with humanity including ourselves and others.

Herein one finds a unique prescription for an optimistic attitude to life, which in turn is conducive to making life more pleasurable and enjoyable.

WHY LOVE?

Of course, the biblical imperative to love others just as we would love our own selves only offers a general directive. What still remains to be answered is, "Why should we love ourselves?" The simple utilitarian answer is that when we love ourselves, and think enough of ourselves and our capacities that we make full use of all the bounty that has been given to us on this earth, we are much better off and our lives are so much the better for it. The melancholy individual who is down on the self would rather not live; the happy, optimistic person cannot wait for the next pleasurable experience, and is actually eager to live. Confronted with a choice of eagerness to live versus readiness to give up, the first alternative is obviously more inviting.

This utilitarian answer, valid as it may be from a narcissistic point of view, can in the long run be somewhat self-defeating, if not altogether so, since its entire focus is on "What's in it for me?" The primary ethic of this life-style evolves around a set of philosophical niceties that are really artificially adhered to in order to bring maximum advantage to the individual. Even the love of others, in such a framework, ultimately is seen as a tool in order to aggrandize to the self all the advantages of bestowing such love.

While this may be preferable to the alternative of neglect and hate of others, or indifference to others, it certainly does not approximate the ideal—a pure, authentic, and genuine love of others and of life itself, no matter what others, and life itself, give in return. One can even extend the utilitarian argument farther, and assert that it is only the individual who loves others without expectation of return for that love bestowed, who actually lives out responsibility according to the lofty ideal.

Practically, one who awaits a reward for all goodness bestowed is likely to be disappointed. A person who lives with expectations of return is quite often dissatisfied with the quantity or quality of the return, and this may lead to the individual's questioning whether it is all worth it. It is therefore best, on a practical level, to give and to share without expectation of reward; to give because giving is a value in and of its own self, whether or not it is reciprocated.

Within the Judaic framework, all the utilitarian arguments are really secondary to a profoundly religious argument for loving oneself, and hence loving others. The love of oneself is not infatuation; instead it points to a sense of detachment of the self towards oneself. It speaks of the capacity to look at oneself and to say, "I like what is there," almost in the same sense as one can look at others and say, "I like what is there." *What is there* is a human being imprinted with a God-given soul; a human being of infinite value and endless potential, potential that literally beckons to be actualized. A more precise understanding of this concept—love of self and others, is perhaps evident in the regulations pertaining to suicide and murder.

Two Sides of Life

It is a well known and basic component of Judaism that murder is strictly prohibited. One is not allowed to murder others.[9] What is not so well appreciated is the fact that one is by the very same logic prohibited from murdering one's own self. Suicide is murder, just as the killing of others is murder.[10] The only difference between murder and suicide is that with murder, the killer and the victim are not one and the same. Thus, after the murder has been perpetrated, the killer, if apprehended, can be prosecuted. However, with regard to suicide, killer and victim are one and the same, so that prosecution is impossible. Also, since in Judaism one is usually not punished merely for attempting a crime unsuccessfully, attempted suicide is also not a prosecutable offense.[11]

What is at work in the suicide prohibition is at work in the murder prohibition. One is not allowed to take other lives, and one is not allowed to take one's own life. Each life is a gift of God placed in this world for the purpose of serving God. The act of taking another person's life and the act of taking one's own life are both invasions of God's province, invasions that steal from God the most precious gift that God has given to this world, life itself.

On the positive side, as the very antithesis to murder, is the obligation to enhance and uphold the lives of others, and to uphold one's own life. This is beautifully expressed in the obligation to "love your neighbor as yourself." The obligation to love is an obligation to enhance, to uplift, to uphold, to support, to ennoble, to encourage, to dignify, to affirm the lives of others and one's own. This too, in the Judaic context, is grounded in our belief that life is a precious gift given to us by God, and as such it must be guarded and nurtured with the care, concern, and love that is commensurate with our appreciation of life's infinite value. In other words, it is our appreciation of the life that has been granted to us by God that should, by definition, preclude depression and melancholy.

FULFILLING LIFE

However, this philosophical reality, rooted in faith, is not enough to guarantee that life will be relatively depression-free. With the philosophical rootedness in faith, the gratitude to God and appreciation of God for having granted life, must also come a sense of direction and purpose. The philosophical awareness is a good starting point, but life embarks from that starting point and must move toward something, someone, or somewhere.

The commandments, we are told, were given in order to shape humankind;[12] or, to transpose this, to give humankind shape and direction. Furthermore, within the Judaic context, the life that has been granted comes only as part of a package. The rest of the package contains those ingredients needed to give life direction and purpose, which are achieved through the study of God's law, the Torah, and observance of God's commandments—referred to as the *mitzvot*.

It is within this framework that one can readily understand the significance of the statement, "God desired to make Israel meritorious, therefore God proliferated for them Torah (to study) and commandments (to actualize)."[13] The study of God's word and the actualization of God's command are the contextual framework within which one realizes one's purpose and direction. For some, the study of God's words may be purpose and direction enough.

However, the ideal, as projected in the Talmud, is that study is great when it leads to action, to good deeds.[14] One cannot remain stultified in the world of theory and dialectic; the theory and dialectic must have practical application and expression. The law, the Judaic legal code, offers a multitude of value possibilities that can be actualized and that are conducive to giving one a sense of purpose and meaning in life. Once imbued with that sense of purpose and meaning through the actualization of God's word, one gives tangible and concrete expression to the philosophical proposition that life is a gift of God. One thus should be able to ward off any possibility that depression may become the motif of a life.

TRUE JOY

Two examples of fulfillment and the direction that they should take are quite instructive in reference to the matter of depression. Both deal with obligations to be joyous, but the actual manner in which they are expressed gives further insight into what the essence of joy really is.

The one instance relates to the obligation to be joyous on the festivals, the pilgrimage holy days of Passover, Pentecost, and Tabernacles (*Pesah, Shavuot,* and *Sukkot*). On these days, there is an obvious religious ambience, creating the spiritual sensitivity to the meaning of the specific festival. This is manifested in the synagogue liturgy, and given further expression in the celebration in the home.

The home celebration includes various delicacies traditional for the occasions, including sanctification with wine, and a sumptuous meal including meat, which under normal circumstances was not part of the regular diet.[15] It would be assumed that an individual who celebrates the festival with proper prayer in the synagogue, and then goes on to an appropriate home celebration including wine and meat, among other festive fare, has properly expressed the obligation to be joyous. Not so, suggests Maimonides, the great Jewish philosopher of the 12th century.

Maimonides, in a very blunt statement, asserts that the individual who celebrates the festivals by indulging the palate, has not really celebrated the festival as much as that person has celebrated his own stomach.[16] There is an obligation to be joyous, but it is not narcissistic joy that we are asked to experience. We are asked to bring others within the scope of the experience, to share the joy, and to experience the joy of sharing. The experience of joy in isolation is more a glorified self-indulgence than it is a religious value. For joy to have a religious value attached to it, it must incorporate sensitivity to others, sensitivity to their own need to experience joy in togetherness.

Another area where joy is an obligation is in the marriage sphere. Here, there is an obligation placed upon the husband to establish the joyfulness of his marital partner, literally "to gladden his wife."[17] A person can be very happy in marriage, and may be ecstatic in his choice of a mate; but that is not the joy that is glorified in Jewish tradition. The essential joy that Judaism desires in the marital context is the joy that the husband creates by making the wife happy.

In both these instances, in the joy of the festival, and in the joy of marriage, it is outer directedness rather than self-aggrandizement which is the ideal. Again, this is not intended to convey that one neglect the self, since awareness of and appreciation of oneself is a basic requisite. What is desired is that one graduates from mere appreciation of the self, and being at ease with oneself, and builds upon that towards extending to others and sharing the self with others.

The idea elaborated upon here is best encapsulated in the famous phrase of Hillel, the noted first century Talmudic sage: "If I am not for myself, who will be for me? But if I am for my own self only, what am I?"[18] First, an individual must take care of the self, must make sure that one is firmly anchored and rooted in life and set toward its purpose. Having achieved this, one cannot remain stultified in self-realization, but must grow outward and embrace others, and thus find that own self reinforced in the process. No better way has been invented to counter depression.

One recalls the famous episode attributed to Alfred Adler, who was once approached by a woman who complained of being depressed. Adler told her to spend the first half hour after awakening, every day for the next 2 weeks, just thinking of ways that she could make other people happy, and he assured her that if she did this, her depression would lift.

THE MOURNING EXPERIENCE

In spite of the fact that depression as a state of mind is not a desirable way of life, it is nevertheless the fact that there are mournful periods in one's life. We have already made reference to the tragic events that almost no one escapes, the death of a parent, a spouse, a sibling, a child, or some other close relative or friend, aside from one's own sickness and eventually impending death. Perhaps the only foolproof way for escaping these tragedies is by dying young. or never being born.[19] Suffering is a component of life. Those who seek to avoid suffering by forming no attachment whatsoever, and therefore never having to mourn a death, deprive themselves of the greatest of all gifts in life, the gift of love.

Aside from this unavoidable sorrow, in the Jewish calendar there are prescribed periods when it is obligatory to be sad. One is a 33-day period between Passover and the Pentecost, a period of semimourning for the tragic loss of life that befell the Jewish people in the past.[20] Another, more intense period, is the 3-week interval between the 17th of Tamuz and 9th of Av, during which the destruction of the Temple in Jerusalem took place.[21] The 17th of Tamuz is a fast day commemorating the first breaches that were made in the wall of Jerusalem.[22] From that date commences a 3-week period in which marriages do not take place, and other forms of semi-mourning are in order.[23]

From the first day of the month of Av, the experience of mourning is deepened, and even normal pleasures such as the eating of meat or the drinking of wine are proscribed, except on the Sabbath.[24] Then, the 9th of Av is itself a day of intense mourning, when one does not sit on an ordinary chair, but close to the ground; eating, drinking, and even the slightest forms of washing are prohibited, as are sexual relations.[25] Even normal speech is curtailed, and greetings among friends are eliminated.[26] If all the laws pertaining to Tishah B'Av (9th of Av) are adhered to, it cannot but produce a somber atmosphere.

Does this in any way contradict the proposed thesis regarding depression? On the contrary: the spirit of melancholy created for the 9th day of Av is rather an affirmation of the present thesis than a contradiction. Historically, it would of course have been preferable that the Jewish people not have to suffer the destruction of the Temple, and not once but twice; they thus would also have been spared the fate of exile. However, these events did take place; and the only way that we can be sensitive to the future of the Jewish people is to be sensitive to their past. Redemption cannot really be experienced unless one understands captivity.

When we are told that whoever mourns for Jerusalem will merit seeing its joy,[27] this is not merely a theological statement, but also a psychological truth. Only a person who can mourn over a loss can appreciate a joy. It is only a person who appreciates the loss of Jerusalem enough to cry over it who can, in the future, experience the triumph of having once again reclaimed Jerusalem. The prescribed period of mourning for the tragedies of the past is an education in history, an enlightenment in emotions and feelings. It is a learning experience, initiating us into the value of feelings of sadness, because it is only through knowing sorrow that we can fully enter into joy.

In Jewish tradition, there is a statement that the messiah was born on Tishah B'Av.[28] In homiletic terms, this means that the redemptive process is generated on the day of greatest melancholy. In psychological terms, this means that we create the potential for true joy only when we fully appreciate the hours of sadness, past and present. In the brain, the pleasure and pain centers are next to one another. What is true physiologically is also true in life experience.

JOY IN CONTEXT

It is worthwhile contemplating a directive in the Talmud relative to the experience of pleasure and joy. It takes the form of a prohibition; the prohibition against filling one's mouth with laughter in this world.[29] This indicates a stricture against feeling complete happiness, happiness with no limitations whatsoever.

The directive balances the entire discussion of depression and joy. It is important to be happy; but that happiness must be rooted in reality, rather than oblivious to it. A person who is completely happy, seeing no reason whatsoever to be sad, is oblivious to the world around him. Historically, it is impossible for a Jewish person to be happy unless he is unaware of, or unconcerned for the tragedies that have been endured in the past, and that continue to be endured in the present.

For any citizen of the world to be totally happy is to ignore the fact of constantly unfolding tragedies: poverty, war, airplane crashes, natural disasters. How can one be a sensitive person, and unreservedly happy at the same time? In this world, that combination is an impossibility. It is in this context that one can appreciate the Talmudic directive, one pertinent not only to the Jewish community, but to the world at large. Happiness is valid, but in a context of awareness.

For the individual who is confronted with a life that seemingly offers no hope of fulfillment, a life depressing in reality and in prospect, suicide, in the Jewish view, is never an option. Life is entrusted to us and we are asked to make the most of it. Beyond that, the tools to make the most of it, the proliferation of study and deed, are actually presented. There is enough confidence that the tools, properly used, will serve to neutralize depression.

In the past, there were individuals who had as their self-appointed task the raising of others out of melancholy. The Talmud tells of sages who met Elijah in the marketplace and asked him if there was anyone there who merited a share in the world to come. At first Elijah did not see anyone; and then he pointed to two individuals. They were approached by the sages and asked what they did to deserve eternity. They replied that they were professionals at cheering up people who felt depressed. They would search out people who were despondent and melancholy, and would, through their own actions, lift up their spirits.[30]

Today it is the psychologists and psychotherapists whom society has entrusted with the task of lifting people out of their depressions. However, in most instances, the procedure takes the form of a functional exercise. Through medication, or behavioral techniques, or some other methodology, the individual is brought out of the depression.

Within the Judaic context, mere freedom from depression is only a fraction of the desired norm, which is to "serve God with joy."[31] That is not achieved merely in the absence of depression; it is achieved through a spirit of optimism and joy, grounded in faith in God, in gratitude and appreciation for having been granted the gift of life, and energized and fueled by the sense of direction and purpose gained by learning God's work and then actualizing it.

5

Experiencing Pleasure

PLEASURE—TWO TYPES

The dictionary offers, among others, two distinct definitions of pleasure. The one defines it as a feeling of being pleased; the second, as worldly or frivolous delight. These two definitions incorporate the extremes in the experiencing of pleasure. Pleasure can be a feeling, a state of being, a manifestation of individual philosophy. It can also be a fleeting experience, an unnatural "high" that obscures reality and gives the individual a temporary and unrealistic sensation.

Although, within Jewish tradition, the experience of pleasure is desirable, this obviously refers to the experience of pleasure within a context. This is best encapsuled in the Talmudic dialectic that alludes to two verses, one viewing happiness as praiseworthy,[1] and the other questioning its value.[2] To resolve this apparent contradiction, the Talmud offers the simple explication that a praiseworthy happiness is the type related to commandment (mitzvah), while happiness of dubious value is dissociated from commandment.[3]

There is a *reality principle* that is associated with the Jewish *plea-*

sure principle. That reality principle affirms that for pleasure to be of ennobling quality, it must be a meaningful pleasure, experienced in a meaning context. In Talmudic terms, this translates as pleasure associated with the fulfillment of a commandment. This is real pleasure, rather than intoxicating pleasure; pleasure that comes from an authentic life joy, experienced in sobriety, and that can be recalled the day after.

Moreover, because it is a pleasure associated with *reasons,* rather than with *causes,* it is more likely to be a pleasure that is a *plateau,* rather than a *peak*. Pleasure as a "high" is apt to be a sudden but transient episode in an otherwise featureless existence, a peak which is surely to be followed by a valley or a hangover.

On the other hand, pleasure that is real and meaningful is that which has enduring and positive aftereffects. The person who is pleased at having performed a good deed, at having helped someone else, is not likely to rest on his laurels, or to see that performance as a rationale for not helping anyone else in the future. At the same time, that feeling of having pleased someone else and done something beneficial, leaves the doer in a pleased state; happy, if not ecstatic, at having been able to help, and at the same time eager to do further good deeds when the opportunity arises, even seeking such opportunities.

The differing forms of pleasure, frivolous delight, and the more lasting feeling of being pleased, are the result of differing approaches to life. Often the individual who seeks out the superficial pleasure is an unhappy individual who tries to camouflage the dissatisfaction with sudden bursts of excitement.

A Matter of the Heart

The behavior syndrome of sudden bursts of high spirits and their consequences is addressed in the well-known Talmudic statement, "Jesting and levity accustom a person to lewdness."[4] *Jesting* may be seen as a form of sarcasm targeting another person. *Levity* is a general lack of seriousness, not directed at any particular individual. These behaviors, jesting and levity, and their concomitants, can adversely affect the individual. Sarcasm and lack of seriousness can lead the person off the value track, toward an imbalanced preoccupation with trivial diversions and a yielding to the emotions of the moment. This is to compensate with momentary gratification for the lack of substantive fulfillment.

The lewdness that may be the consequence of this type of frivolous behavior is really a sensual expression void of meaning, indiscriminately expressed without concern for or sensitivity to the other partner in the experience. It is humanly degrading, and certainly devoid of true significance. In all the Judaic literature which spells out the legitimate ways for individuals to be happy, to be pleased, this is not the kind of happiness and pleasure that is advocated.

The Divine Presence, we are told, rests only on the glad heart.[5] Why the accent on *glad heart,* rather than on glad person? The heart is conceived as the seat of human emotions, that unique part of the human being expressive of all that is good and exalted. Other organs of the body may be satisfied; pleasure sensations indicating satisfaction may be transmitted to the brain through the experience of pleasure; but this does not compare in quality to the happiness of the heart.

The happiness of the heart is a steady, human happiness, a lasting and meaningful expression of the individual's being imbued with those values that make life meaningful for the self and for others. Judaism wants every individual to be happy, and to experience pleasure, with the aim that the individual should feel pleased at being in the world, a part of the world; grateful for having been placed on earth in order to enjoy the bounty that God has bestowed on the world, and in order to help others to enjoy God's bounty. The cruelty of others has too often obstructed this process, yet this should not detract from its validity.

Undoubtedly, even within this context, there will be pleasure "peaks," but they will rise from the plateau of a pleased *state,* to which they will subside. This is in contradistinction to the "highs" of pleasure that are an escape from acedia or melancholy, and temporary at that.

PLEASURE IN SERVING

Pleasure, and the attendant feelings of being pleased, happy, optimistic, affirmative, of being eager to immerse oneself in life—in causes, in ideals, and in enhancing the lives of others—that pleasure is a state of being, as well as an attitude; it is a distinct approach to life.

When one is pleased, one does not begrudge others their own joy, and one does not envy the material possessions of others. Who is rich? asks the Talmud. The answer is, the one who is happy with his portion.[6] One takes life and the unchangeables of life as givens, and tries to build upon these in an optimistic and affirmative spirit, thus to enhance life. One who is pleased with the self and with life usually extends that feeling to others, and is indeed able to "receive all people with cheerfulness."[7]

In the religious context, the behavior formula is relatively simple and straightforward. All our deeds should be for the sake of God;[8] our entire life is a life of service to God, and that service, we are told, should be within the framework of the commandment, "Serve God with joy."[9] That is the all-encompassing environmental mood that should prevail in one's life.

Historically, it has been pointed out, there are times in the calendar year when a feeling of mourning and depression becomes mandatory. These are interludes in a life otherwise colored by joy and happiness. It is interesting to note in this regard that on Tishah B'Av, the 9th day of Av, the most melancholy day in the Jewish calendar, commemorating the destruction of both the first and second Temples—and in our own time seen as a day in which mourning for more contemporary destructions of total Jewish communities is observed—on that day of Tishah B'Av, the study of God's Torah is forbidden.[10]

The only items of the Torah that are permitted to be studied on that day are those that relate to the laws of mourning, or the laws of Tishah B'Av itself, as well as the more melancholy portions of the prophets and the history of the more tragic periods of Jewish history.[11] Even in those areas of study that are permitted, the law states that the study must be of a surface nature, rather than more profound and concentrated. The reason for all this is that the words of the Torah, God's commands, are described as upright, and gladdening the heart.[12] Since Tishah B'Av is the one day in the year when we are not allowed to be glad, we are therefore not allowed to study God's Torah in depth.

PLEASURE AS NORM

This regulation projects two very important notions concerning the concepts of pleasure and joy. Firstly, Tishah B'Av, by virtue of its being singled out as the exception, also speaks eloquently about all the other days of the year, which are the rule. If on Tishah B'Av the rule is sadness and melancholy, for the rest of the year the rule is joy and optimism.

Secondly, the fact that Torah study is forbidden on Tishah B'Av because it gladdens the heart, is also indicative of the mood that should prevail in the study of Jewish law and lore. Properly approached, the study of Judaic texts is fulfilling and inspiring, affording an ultimate form of pleasure—the pleasure of having further probed into the meaning of God's word, and thus better enabled to actualize God's values.

The study of commandments is described as gladdening the heart. The fulfillment of what is studied—the escalation of theory into practice—should also, by definition, gladden the heart. Thus, though there are specific commandments in which joy is a requisite, such as in the celebration of the festivals, or in marriage, the other commandments, being fulfillments of God's word, must also be inspired by a joyous spirit.

It turns out that within the Judaic context, holiness is not achieved through separating from life, from its pleasures and delights, and locking oneself away in a world of privation, deprivation, and denial. Rather, holiness is achieved through experiencing pleasure in a meaningful way, through escalating into transcending exercises what to many may be self-serving experiences.[13] Judaism desires not that pleasure be eliminated from life, but that pleasure be transmuted into a unique combination of the physical and spiritual dimensions, which mutually nourish each other, and raise pleasure to a real, meaningful, and lasting state of being.

Relative to this Judaic understanding of pleasure, there is a unique piece of legislation which focuses on an interesting perspective in the experience of pleasure. That legislation is the halakhah, or law, that we should not, indeed are not allowed, to mix one joyous occasion with another.[14] Translated, this means that in Jewish law one cannot schedule a marriage ceremony for a festival day or even for the intermediate days of the festival.[15]

One would think that the festival, by definition a joyous time— indeed a time when joy is mandatory and all-encompassing—would be ideal for a wedding. After all, in a period which is guaranteed to be festive, the marriage itself would be immeasurably uplifted. Nevertheless, the law says no and insists that marriage take place on a day in which joy is not a religious obligation.

Since the festival is a peak occasion of joy, as distinct from everyday happiness, which is a plateau-type of joy, and the wedding is also a peak moment, the law, in effect, suggests that two such experiences coinciding detract from each other. Rather than try to fuse the experiencing of the festival and of the marriage, the law prescribes that we nurture each of these moments in their full glory. Neither occasion should be compromised by a deliberate synchrony, or placed in mutual competition.

This regulation, standardized as it is within Jewish life, bespeaks the insistence that a pleasure be accorded its full due, and valued in its own right.

GAMBLING

According to Talmudic law, a gambler is unfit to testify in court.[16] One reason suggested for this is that the gambler does not contribute to the habitation of the world.[17] Obviously, such reasoning suggests that we are dealing not with an occasional gambler, but with a professional gambler, one whose life is spent at the gambling tables or at the racetrack.

Occasional gambling, in this view, is not condemned. As many have pointed out, there is precious little difference between an individual who bets on a horse and one who bets on a stock. The one is called a gambler, the other is called an investor. But essentially, the dynamics of both types of risk-taking are the same.

The Talmud, however, does condemn, and in blunt terms, an individual whose only vocation is to use funds to bet, and to try to win through the betting. Such an individual does not contribute to the welfare of society, is not involved in any gainful employment, and is fundamentally divorced from the human endeavor.

The habitual gambler certainly is not lacking for thrills. The gambler not only enjoys the occasional winning, but the act of gambling itself. The gambler, assuming that he is well enough endowed financially, is probably perfunctorily happy, enjoying the ups and the downs, the thrills and the drama, the uncertainty and the possibility. The gambler experiences pleasure, but it is unprincipled pleasure—pleasure without principle.

The gambler therefore has no right to make any statement that will affect the destiny of other human beings. The Talmud states clearly that only those who are involved in greater human destiny, in helping society through some form of positive contribution, have a right to testify in court.

This regulation places the concept of pleasure, and its role in life, into a strict legal framework. The experience of pleasure is desired, and desirable; but it must be a pleasure that is more than self-centered, and that enhances others even as it enhances the self.

DRINKING RESPONSIBLY

There are some unique forms of experiencing pleasure that pose problems. In general terms, these are pleasures that are intoxicating or harmful. In the first category, that of intoxicant, alcohol and drugs are prime examples. In the category of pleasure that is harmful, cigarette smoking comes to the fore as the most salient example.

Wine is considered, by the Talmudists, to have both positive and negative qualities. On the positive side, wine can induce happiness; wine itself is identified with happiness. Thus, there is no joy except with wine.[18] Wine is seen as having the capacity to help an individual get over trying times; wine was not created for this world except to comfort mourners.[19] Wine also seems to have been identified as an intellectual stimulant.[20] Wine is a relaxant.[21]

Wine is considered beneficial for the entire body.[22] It stabilizes the bodily evacuation process, straightens out one's posture, and brightens one's eyes, according to the Talmud.[23] Wine is judged to be helpful in producing milk for a nursing mother.[24] Wine is good not only as a drink; it is also good as a form of oil for individuals who may have to massage ailing limbs.[25]

On the negative side, wine can, of course, cause drunkenness, with all the attendant problems.[26] Wine can cause an individual to vomit up all food.[27] Wine can be degrading, especially when one loses control because of the wine.[28]

It is readily apparent that the advantages deriving from wine are so many, that the Talmud surely could not espouse abstention or temperance. Yet the dangers of alcohol consumption are obvious now, and were obvious then. How then, are the two properties of wine reconciled?

From the Talmudic view, the answer is straightforward. Too much wine is detrimental to the person, and wine in moderation is beneficial.[29] In the passage concerning wine gladdening the heart of the individual,[30] the Talmud sees in it alternate readings, from which it derives the rule that if a person is meritorious, wine gladdens; but if not, it destroys.[31] In other words, one is obliged to exercise control and to limit consumption, allowing the wine to have its maximum beneficial effect. Excess can result in destructive consequences.

Wine is associated with every joyous celebration. A cup of wine is employed to usher in the Sabbath,[32] to pronounce blessing at a wedding,[33] at the culmination of a circumcision ceremony,[34] at the ceremony effecting the redemption of the firstborn.[35]

On the festival of Passover, four cups of wine are part of the basic observance of the Passover Seder,[36] the Seder being the initiating meal and experience of the Passover festival. The four cups are identified with the four languages of redemption.[37] This conveys a connection between the drinking of wine and freedom. Considering that within Judaism freedom is closely linked with responsibility, in that one is free not in a libertarian way but free in exercising responsibility, the connection of wine with freedom is meaningful.

Wine used properly is beneficial; wine abused is harmful. Inherent in the use of wine, therefore, is the counterpoise of freedom and responsibility. One is free to drink, but responsible to drink in proper measure. Wine symbolizes the attitude that we are not to withdraw from the pleasures of the world; we are to partake of those pleasures in moderation, so that the pleasure experiences are sober and coherent. One exercises freedom in restraint, in being watchful against exceeding reasonable limits. Through such free-willed expression, one exercises responsibility for the consequences of overindulgence, even at the same time that one indulges.

Drinking in High Places

Referring to wine, a unique biblical directive is given to the priests (*Kohanim*; singular, *Kohen*), "Wine and strong drink you shall not drink, you nor your sons with you, when you go into the tent of appointed meeting. . . ."[38] The priests, who ministered in the Temple, were enjoined from entering to serve when in an inebriated state. Any service performed in such a state was looked upon as a capital offense.[39] This regulation applied not only to wine but also to any drink that intoxicates.[40]

The priests were singled out, which itself leads to a number of questions, the first being: why is there legislation concerning drunkenness only with regard to the priest? Surely anyone who brought a sacrifice to the Temple should have been bound by the same explicit restrictions. Secondly, since we are obliged to serve God with gladness,[41] and taking into account that wine makes glad the heart of the human being,[42] it would almost follow logically that priests *should* drink wine upon entering to perform their service. After all, they are obliged to minister in gladness.

It is undoubtedly true that wine would make the priest glad, but it would not give the priest a *reason* to be glad; only a *cause*. In the realm of causes, there are even better ways to make an individual happy. All one need do is to attach electrodes to the brain's pleasure center and send electrical impulses to stimulate the pleasure sense. In such a setup, one could feel pleasure sensations at any time. Why is it that in the pursuit of happiness we have not argued for the electrode system? Simply because the human, whether aware of it or not, is concerned more with having a reason to be happy, and not merely with a cause for happiness. With a reason, the human being *is* happy; with only a cause, one is *made* to be happy. Authentic human nature has almost willy-nilly triumphed over uncontrolled human desire. The human nature yearns for the true fulfillment of self that will only automatically, and merely as a side effect, make one happy.

Drinking wine as a path to gladness is a mechanistic approach to a situation that demands the human dimension. Reaching a state of joy through the fulfillment of a human task, such as philanthropy, or approximating gladness on the threshold of performing the inspiring duty of service in the Temple, are human accomplishments achieved through the exercise of one's will.

There are two ways to reach the roof of a building. One can either take the elevator or walk the stairs. By elevator one is elevated, by the stairs one elevates one's self. Through wine, one is elevated to the roof, though in fact the individual has done nothing to merit the height. Through internal human endeavor one climbs the ladder to the roof, to the heights of human fulfillment; it is a height consistent with the true state of the individual.

The priest (Kohen) is singled out, and stands out as that individual, working in the summit of Jewish edifices, the Temple, who is called upon to reach that height by climbing, not by being artificially catapulted. The priest is a prototype; the Jewish people, as a kingdom of *priests* in the service of God,[43] are likewise asked to use the same height pyschology as that asked of the priest. The hallmark of this height psychology is a sober intoxication with life and its purpose.

THE DIVIDING LINE

The verse immediately following that enjoining the priest from having wine before ministering in the Temple reads, "And that you may differentiate between the holy and the ordinary . . ."[44] This exhortation, seemingly unconnected with the previous verse, relates to the very basis of the wine or drug intoxicating experiences. One naturally desires a high, a peak experience, a mystical involvement with the world, even with God. Quite often the thin dividing line between the sacred and the ordinary escapes human cognition. What difference is there how one feels euphoria?

At times, we are subjected to philosophical intrigue in the debate about whether the end justifies the means. Judaism emphasizes not only the end but also, very definitely, how one reaches it. There are no short cuts to meaning or sanctity.

Heaven is not reached by a flight of chemical spontaneity, but by the steadily mounting degrees of human fulfillment. Noteworthy here is the dream of Jacob, who saw in a vision not only the heavens; he also saw a ladder anchored in earth and reaching the heavens.[45] The way to heaven, to Godliness, is by the steps of a ladder; the sure way of getting there is by climbing.

There is a thin dividing line between the sacred and the ordinary, a dividing line of means. The end is meaningless, and is not a human achievement if the means have not been human. Thus, one who recites the prayer when in a state of drunkenness is as one who serves idols.[46] To induce a holy state, a state of prayer, through artificial means, is to make an end of the means, to worship a condition rather than to work for it. This is tantamount to idolatry.

The evidence with regard to hard drugs would convince any sane individual to shun their use. However, there is some controversy with regard to the "soft stuff," marijuana and hashish; some insist they are harmless, others maintain they have deleterious effects. It may very well be that one is likely to find difficulty in defending the position that it is wrong to take soft drugs. Users are apt to contend there is nothing wrong with taking them, or to insist that they are just as harmful as wine. Indeed there can be no question that wine in excess is harmful.

With regard to both wine and drugs the question that should be asked is not, "What is wrong with taking them?"; but rather, "What is right in taking them?" We are bidden to be holy, which in simple terms means that we are obliged to make life as meaningful as possible and to elicit everlasting value from every minute of life. Thus, even if there may possibly be nothing wrong with taking this drug or that alcoholic drink, there may be nothing right about it either, and ultimately this is what counts. We should not be satisfied just with not doing what is wrong; we should insist on doing what is right, what is meaningful.

SMOKING

Cigarette smoking is a form of pleasure that has a harmful effect on health. The question that remains to be answered is whether smoking can be permitted, since it does give pleasure, though at great expense.

Research into cigarette smoking has confirmed that it is the main cause of lung cancer, the most important cause of chronic obstructive lung disease (emphysema), and a significant factor in the incidence of coronary heart disease, cancer of the larynx, and cancer of the bladder.

Cigarette smoking has become as important a cause of death as the great epidemic diseases such as cholera, tuberculosis, and typhoid. In effect, with all the attempts, there still is no such thing as a safe cigarette. Cigarette smoking is a unique form of self-destruction, suicide on the installment plan.

There are many who justify their smoking with the specious argument from fatalism. They will only live as long as God wants anyway; so what difference does it make if they smoke? Aside from ignoring the pollutant effect of smoking on others, this argument is superficial theology. Granted that the years of our life may be predetermined, yet who would be so bold as to declare that this predetermination is etched in stone? Can one walk through fire or jump off a bridge with the rationalization that if one's years are predetermined, any suicidal act will be survived? May we eat ourselves into obesity with the assurance that God's allotment of years will guarantee us longevity even as we squander our health?

A well thought out theology would impose upon us an obligation to sanctify life in quality in order to assure its quantity. The fitness buffs of this generation come closer to a balanced religiosity than do the smokers.

Suicide is clearly forbidden in Jewish law. It is an instance of nonprosecutable murder, as has been pointed out, since victimizer and victim are one and the same. But the same logic that prohibits the murder of others forbids the murder of the self; we are simply not permitted to destroy life, life being a gift of God *entrusted* to us, rather than being ours. We are trustees, not referees. The biblical exhortation, "But for your own life I will require a reckoning. . ."[47] applies to any suicidal act, and cigarette smoking seems eminently to qualify in that category. Because life is sacred, intentionally placing oneself in danger is also explicitly prohibited.[48] ". . . Take heed unto yourself and take care of your life. . .",[49] "Be exceedingly heedful of your selves. . ."[50] are far-reaching imperatives to avoid endangering one's existence.

Included in the scope of this prohibition are numerous actions, such as drinking from uncovered water lest a snake dropped venom into it, or putting money into one's mouth lest it carry the germs of someone with an infectious disease, or just human perspiration, which in itself is harmful; and also walking near a leaning wall or over a shaky bridge.[51] Maimonides expressly dismisses the right of the individual to say "What concern is it to others if I want to put myself in danger?"[52] This is a primary denial of the sanctity and inviolability of life.

UNRESOLVED DEBATE

It would seem that the permissibility of cigarette smoking according to Jewish law should be beyond debate, but in fact the matter has lamentably not yet been adequately resolved.

The matter of whether smoking is itself forbidden has been subjected to various Judaic legal pronouncements, all of them unanimous in discouraging smoking, but nowhere near unanimity on whether smoking is in fact legally prohibited.

Rabbi David HaLevi, the Sephardic Chief Rabbi of Tel Aviv, raised quite a furor in Israel when in 1976 he declared that cigarette smoking was forbidden according to Jewish law. His pronouncement, widely covered in the Israeli press, was greeted with an incongruous reaction from one Rabbi who claimed that life was difficult enough as it was for the Jewish people, and that Rabbi HaLevi was doing no one a favor by adding to the list of prohibitions. As if Rabbi HaLevi's purpose was to make life difficult for the Jews! Those who forbid smoking consider it a threat to life. The prohibition is an affirmation of life—not a denial.

One noted sage states that since so many smoke, we rely on the fact that God watches over the simple,[53] but there is definitely no prohibition from the point of view of danger to health.[54] Given the overwhelming evidence of the physiological effects of smoking and their endangerment to health, it is hard to establish grounds for allowing smoking.

To claim, as some have, that if we prohibit smoking, we should prohibit crossing the street, because statistics show that many people who cross the street get run over by cars,[55] is obviously a specious argument. There is a statistical connection between crossing the street and being hit, but not a causal connection. Cigarette smoking has been more than implicated in the incidence of lung cancer, respiratory diseases, and other body ailments; not merely statistically, but causally.

The argument that the effects of smoking are reversible, in that one can clean up the body system from its contaminants within a year or two, even after prolonged heavy smoking, should also not affect Judaic legal judgment. First, it is doubtful whether all the effects of the smoking can be erased. Secondly, the Talmud lists many foods that should not be eaten because they are harmful, as well as behaviors that should not be indulged in because of their effects, even though one could instantly break the habit and restore the body's equilibrium.

For example, the Talmud states that one should not sit too long because excessive sitting aggravates one's abdominal troubles (piles), one should not stand for a prolonged period because this is injurious to the heart, and one should not walk too much because excessive walking is harmful to the eyes. Rather, one should spend one third of the time sitting, one third standing, and one third walking.[56] But it is not instantaneously that one develops any of these effects. They are rather a cumulative result of a repeated practice. The regulation holds, although one could sit, or stand, or walk too much and still correct these habits in time. Thus the reversibility of what is intrinsically not right does not make it permissible.

There is understandable reluctance explicitly to prohibit an activity to which a great portion of the population, many of them God-fearing people, have become habituated. But the magnitude of the hazards linked to smoking should overcome this reluctance. Smoking is a pleasure that eventually turns to tragedy, and tragic pleasures have no place in Judaic life. Pleasure, meaning, and life itself are inextricably linked with each other.

6

Enjoyment of Life

BEAUTY AND TRADITION

There are many experiences and fulfillments in life from which we derive benefit. Such benefits, or enjoyments, are in themselves desirable and gratifying.

Foremost among experiences that impart meaningful pleasure are the study and the actualization of God's word. Yet, the Talmud asserts that the commandments were not given for us to derive benefit therefrom. What is the meaning of this statement?

Essentially, it means that this is not the ultimate purpose of the commandments. The ultimate purpose is to give direction, goal, and meaning to one's life. Direction, purpose, and meaning are of course best realized in an environment of enjoyment, as any teacher or student would testify. However, the enjoyment is not an end in itself, but a means towards a higher goal.

In the awareness of the ultimate goal, it is nevertheless true that enjoyment, pleasure, and the experience of beauty are essential elements of life. After all, if we are asked to glorify God,[1] and there are certain observances through which this glorification is rendered, we must perfect a sense of what is fitting in order respectfully to fulfill such commandments.

For example, the citron, or *etrog,* that is used on the festival of the Tabernacles, must, by biblical fiat, be *beautiful.*[2] We are given strict legal parameters establishing what is a minimally acceptable citron, and also other general guidelines for what makes a citron beautiful.[3] It may be true that beauty is in the eyes of the beholder; this applies essentially when an individual desires to establish a relationship, or to purchase an object.

However, with regard to a citron, there are specific guidelines, so that the criterion of what is beautiful is not left to individual whim. Within the parameters clearly delineated, there is, of course, scope for variance. Some people like a bigger citron, others a smaller one. What is important is that the choice be one which the individual considers beautiful, in the context of what is legislated as "beautiful."

The Tabernacle, or sukkah, in which one sits for the Sukkot Tabernacle festival can be a simple shack made of wood, or it can be a more presentable abode, with ample decoration and many of the amenities that one would find in a normal home.[4] The luxury of a sukkah more than adequately adorned is an application of the principle of beauty to the fulfillment of a commandment.

Simplicity and Beauty

One may, in the purchase of the prayer shawl, or the phylacteries, buy something simple, or something exquisite. The same is true of the parchment scrolls that make up the mezuzah that is affixed to the doorpost of the home. One can purchase parchment scrolls that are minimally acceptable; one can seek out more exquisitely written and meticulously detailed script.

The Sabbath table bears many items that have religious significance, including the wine cup over which santification is recited, the plate holding the two loaves of bread, and the covering for the two loaves. Some may claim that there is a thin line separating beauty from ostentation; but it is nevertheless true that the Sabbath projects itself much more positively with a wine cup made of silver, silver plate, or metal, than it would if the sanctification (kiddush) were recited over a styrofoam cup of wine.

Individuals who cannot afford anything but a styrofoam cup assuredly have no choice; but those who can afford it should give the desired significance to the Sabbath by purchasing appropriate instruments for Sabbath observance. This applies to practically all areas of Jewish observance that call for tangible manifestations. The value that is attached to the commandment is in some measure reflected in the way that the commandment's palpable form of expression is glorified and beautified.

In the sanctuary, the ark containing the commandments was actually made of two substances, acacia *wood*, overlaid on the inside and the outside by *gold*.[5] The combination is unique in that it delivers the message that we should appropriate to God's home our best resources, at the same time maintaining an awareness that humility also belongs to God's home. Hence wood, symbolizing the humility of the earth source, is combined with the royal splendor of gold.

Throughout history, the concept of the synagogue, starting with the portable Tabernacle, continuing with the Temple, and then with various synagogues, has inspired some of the most beautiful structures. Of one particular variation of the Temple, the Talmud states that whoever had not seen it had not really seen a beautiful structure.[6]

Awareness and appreciation of what is beautiful thus is elementary to Jewish life.

ARTISTIC EXPRESSION

Yet, one is left with a perception that in certain aesthetic areas, Judaism did not excel as in other fields, such as medicine.[7] Although synagogue and religious art, in terms of arks, center stage (*bima*), wine cups, spice boxes, marriage contracts, and other religious items, had flourished over the generations, art for its own sake had not flourished in like measure. At least, that is the impression.

Many reasons had been suggested for this seeming gap in Jewish cultural expression. There was the feeling among some that Jewish artistic endeavor simply was a waste of time, since it did not contribute to religious expression. Why waste time drawing pictures, or painting landscapes, when that time could be used to construct religious artifacts, or to study, or to perform good deeds? Of course, this is not to suggest that every individual in the Jewish community was preoccupied with such religious expression. This only explains, in some measure, why the community would not have encouraged such endeavor.

Another explanation proposed for the dearth of Jewish artists is that the prohibition against creating forms, one of the Ten Commandments, may have stood in the way of much artistic expression. The biblical commandment, that one not make any form of human being or animal, has been variously interpreted, usually as a prohibition against creating a complete figuration, lest that figuration become an idol that is worshipped.[8] This would obviously severely limit the artistic individual, who would be quite restricted in the subject matter that could be applied to canvas.

Recently, however, evidence has been discovered which casts much doubt upon the previously held assumptions. Jews did engage in various forms of artistic expression, and were quite influential over the centuries. Ironically, because art was so Hebraic, Jewish involvement was restricted during the great era of European painting. The painting was for decorating non-Jewish institutions, and Jews were prevented from being involved.[9]

Once the connection between art and the ecclesiastical was loosened, Jewish artistic expression began to flourish. In this generation, religiously acceptable art in the form of kinetic configurations has come to the fore as a uniquely Jewish form.[10]

Whatever the explanation may be for the paucity of Jewish artists and art, or however valid may be the claim that Jews were not involved in art, these do not negate the fact that in general, Judaism appreciates beauty, and integrates the ideal of beauty into religious life.

THE BEAUTY OF NATURE

Apart from created or manufactured beauty, there is, of course, the natural beauty of the world. With regard to the experiencing of such beauty, when viewing majestic heights, rivers, streams, mountains, or oceans, one is obliged to recite a blessing extolling God for having placed such wonders in the world.[11] One who sees blossoming trees is likewise obliged to thank God for having given such bounty to the world.[12] If one sees beautiful trees, one thanks God for having placed such beauty in the world.[13] If, farther on, one sees a tree even more beautiful, that same blessing is recited again.[14]

Every month, a blessing on the new moon, as it reappears after having gone out of sight, is recited.[15] In the 28-year solar cycle, when that cycle is renewed, a great celebration amid blessing takes place.[16] For the natural phenomena thunder and lightning, there are blessings to be recited,[17] as there is upon seeing a rainbow.[18]

Thus, not only is the admiration of natural beauty permitted and encouraged, it is even incorporated into the vast expanse of religious observance.

Yet, the Talmud states: "One who is walking by the way in study, and interrupts the study to exclaim 'how beautiful is this tree!' or 'how beautiful is this field!' is regarded by scripture as having forfeited one's soul."[19]

This may seem to disparage enjoyment of nature. But, given all that has been noted regarding the obligation to bless and thank God for nature's beauty, this cannot be the intent. Rather, one reads in this comment a placing of the admiration of nature into its proper context.

Everything in this world, the heavens and the earth, the sun and the moon, the trees and the fields, manifest the greatness and majesty of God. Nevertheless, this should not develop into an equivalence. There is profound significance in everything, but not everything is the same. There is a scale of values; there are priorities and levels of importance.

One who is walking by the way in study and interrupts to exclaim, "How beautiful is this tree," while affirming the majesty of God in the world, has still made a priority substitution of nature over Torah study. Admiring nature is a part of appreciating the beauty of the world, but is not commensurate with Torah study. Nature is God's work, but the Torah is God's formula for life. Thus, interrupting Torah to admire nature is a value distortion.

BEAUTY AND THE GODLY

The Talmudic comment concludes by declaring that the individual who makes this value distortion is regarded by scripture as having forfeited his soul. It is unclear which verse in scripture is the proof-text for this, but it would seem that *scripture in general* makes this observation. It is in the very nature of the importance of scripture.

One who relegates scripture to second place to nature by allowing nature to distract from Torah meditation, scripture itself sees this as rejection of the very concept of scripture's cruciality to life, as the most vital of all human pursuits. Subordinating this fundamental to admiration of nature denies the primary importance of scripture. It is *as if* one has forfeited one's soul, because in relegating God's word and eternal values to a secondary position, one has denied their essentiality to life, and has thus compromised the value actualization indispensable to a meaningful life.

The admiration of beauty, natural beauty, is an absolute requirement; but it is a requirement, obligation, and value that must take its proportional place among other values more primary and ultimately more significant.

This perspective is highlighted in the story of R. Samson Raphael Hirsch, who gave to his students this rationale for his planned trip to Switzerland: "When I stand shortly before the Almighty, I will be held answerable to many questions: 'Did you transact business with integrity? Did you study Torah with regularity?! But what will I say when — and I'm sure to be asked: 'Shimshon, and did you see My Alps?' "[20]

The obligation to express praise to God upon seeing that which is beautiful extends also to human beings. One who sees a beautiful male or female, should bless and thank God that such beauty has been placed in this world.[21] One also recites a special blessing upon meeting great scholars, or on seeing royalty.[22]

Of the blessing recited on seeing a beautiful individual, there is a clear distinction between *admiring* that beauty — seeing in it a Godly gift — and eyeing that beauty in lust or envy. The lust reaction is not what is referred to in the tradition that one recite a blessing.[23]

The blessing is recited to God; it praises God for beauty that exists. It is a *transcending* act — rather than a self-serving act of personal gratification or even sensual expression. The "staring" type of looking is condemned in Jewish tradition.[24] Staring is not only a capitulation to one's passions, but also makes the other a mere object, to satisfy one's own needs or desires.

In Jewish tradition, one is not even allowed to stare at the sexual characteristics of one's wife.[25] One is obliged to love one's mate as a unique individual, and not to analyze the anatomy, as if the wife were a piece of merchandise that is more valuable if it is in flawless condition. There is a greater beauty than that of the body, and that is the beauty of soul. It is in this direction, the beauty of soul, that the human being's focus should be fixed.

THE MUSICAL EXPERIENCE

Another of the keen enjoyments of life, one that addresses not the eyes but the ears, is music. Music has always been part and parcel of Judaic prayer expression. Many of the most profound biblical prayers were in the form of song.[26] Music was an intrinsic part of the Temple ritual. To the present day, prayer is not only the saying of words, but the singing of songs and of hymns.

Outside the context of prayer, music plays other significant roles. It is a soothing sensation that can calm, tranquilize, and even inspire. The prophets would be made receptive to prophecy through musical evocation.[27] Music is such an effector of a happy mood that an individual in mourning for one of the seven close relatives may not listen to music.[28]

For the 33 days of semimourning between Passover and Pentecost (Shavuot), one refrains from enjoying music.[29] Likewise, during the 3-week period between the 17th of Tamuz and the 9th of Av, when the destruction of the two Temples is commemorated in many ways, one of the forms of mourning observed is abstaining from listening to music.[30] Obviously, by implication, in other periods of the year which are not mournful, music is desirable, inspiriting and inspirational.[31]

Musical, unlike artistic expression, was not subject to much restrictive difficulties. Musically, Judaism has excelled over the centuries, particularly in the portable stringed instruments. In the period of Diaspora, Jews lived an especially precarious existence, not knowing today where they would be tomorrow; instruments had to be portable. It is therefore eminently logical that they should excel more in such instruments as the violin, as opposed to the piano. Violins one can carry, pianos one cannot.

Among great contemporary violinists, so many who are Jewish come to mind—Elman, Heifetz, Menuhin, Oistrakh, Perlman and

Stern. This is not to say that excellence has not evolved in other instrumental traditions. On the piano, among others, are Rubinstein and
Horowitz; and a multitude of composers and conductors of Jewish origin have made significant contributions to the musical repertoire of the
world.[32]

It is obvious that music, since it did not involve the creation of any
forms that could lead to idolatry, did not suffer the same consequences
as art, and generally was allowed free expression and adaptation into the
Jewish life-style.

LEISURE TIME

Aside from the enjoyment of life associated with experiencing
beauty, whether artistic or musical, there is another enjoyment that is
not the experience of any particular pleasure, but rather the contentment
of just letting oneself rest, the body and the senses. This nonpressure in-
terlude is commonly referred to as leisure time; time to relax, free from
anxiety, stress, even activity.

Generally, having nothing to do, sitting idly, is seen as detrimental
to human growth. In fact, idleness leads to idiocy,[33] or alternately, to
destructive behavior.[34] The idleness referred to is surely the type that is
more all-encompassing than merely an occasional rest or vacation. It
speaks of an idleness that is characteristic of one's life, a situation in
which one has no goals or aspirations, and every day is frittered away.

Obviously, the human being who works hard needs time off to replenish the resources. In the Judaic scheme of things, 6 days are rele-
gated for working, and the seventh day is a day of cessation, known as
Shabbat, the Sabbath. The biblical view that 6 days are for work and
one day is for cessation is seen as a dual obligation, an obligation to
work on the six and to cease on the seventh.[35]

That cessation on the seventh day, which becomes a day of relaxation from work, is not designed to be an empty day, in which one does
nothing. For the 6 days one works physically; the seventh day is more
spiritual in emphasis. Then one can contemplate the significance of
what has transpired during the week; one can give meaning to one's life,
a meaning that one may have a difficult time formulating during the in-

tensive work cycle of the week. The Sabbath should be the day one focuses on the purpose of all the work one puts into life.

SABBATH REST

The Sabbath is a day of prohibitions that enjoin many forms of activity, most of them in the "materially creative" category. However, these restrictions are not ends in themselves. Instead, through the atmosphere the restrictions create, the positive fulfillment associated with the Sabbath, spiritual replenishment and meaningful contemplation, is made possible.[36]

In Talmudic terms, the idea that the prohibitive and affirmative aspects of the Sabbath were transmitted simultaneously[37] imparts the message that the prohibitions are only a part of a total fulfillment. It is through adherence to the prohibitions that the affirmation is possible; authentic affirmation of the Sabbath cannot unfold unless the prohibitions are scrupulously observed. Sabbath prohibitions and Sabbath affirmations are parts of a whole, and cannot exist, philosophically or in real life, independent of each other.

The destructive capacity of too much leisure, and too little work, is projected in the biblical flood story. According to tradition, the fate of that generation was sealed through their engaging in petty larceny, in stealing less than a penny's worth from their neighbors, so that cumulatively they inflicted misery, though no single theft warranted taking the perpetrator to court.[38] The question is, why did that generation degenerate to such base behavior?

It is suggested that one of the advantages bestowed upon that generation was a weather cycle of eternal springtime, with no winter-summer fluctuations, and only a once-in-40-years plantation cycle,[39] affording an abundance of spare time to be filled. Unfortunately, the free time was not put to good use, and instead, in frustration at having no direction, the people resorted to destructive behavior for its own sake. It was this form of depravity that brought on the flood and its consequences.

Interestingly, immediately after the flood, a corrective measure was instituted, with weather cycles of fall, winter, spring, summer, a more regular plantation and harvest, and heat and cold, integrated into the human life cycle.[40] This was to preclude the danger of too much spare time, and the consequences that had previously developed. Having to spend much of every year working literally by the sweat of his brow to guarantee sustenance, the human being was no longer able to squander so much time.

There is an important lesson here concerning the leisure-time pursuits, which seem to be a modern day penchant. Leisure is useful and necessary, especially for individuals who work in high-stress jobs. However, too much leisure can be destructive and have harmful affects on the individual and on society as a whole.

THE LEISURE CONTEXT

Essentially, the matter of leisure-time pursuits is one of attitude. There are those who work feverishly in order to have leisure activity, and those who pursue leisure activity in order to have the energy to be productive in their work afterwards. The question of which is the means and which the end is important to the individual's basic philosophical outlook on life.

Those who work in order to have the leisure to laze around are basically not committed to working on improving themselves and the world, and would, if they had a choice, not work at all. Those who see leisure as the time to recharge their batteries so that they can work more energetically, see leisure as a means, and work as a primary necessity for a viable existence.

The Talmud considers morning sleep among those things that drive a person out of the world.[41] This does not refer to the occasional "sleeping in," but to a more habitual form of laziness in which an individual has nothing significant enough to do to merit waking up early in the morning, to get a head start on the day.

The enjoyment of relaxation is certainly a desirable, if not a necessary ingredient in the totality of life. But, as with other pleasures, it needs to be placed in its proper focus; into a meaning context in which leisure is not escalated to an end in itself, but is seen as part and parcel of a meaningful life-style.

With all due deference (not much is due, to be sure) to the culture of narcissism, there is hardly a more meaningful enjoyment that can be experienced by the human being than of making life more pleasurable for others. Without mandating that free time be a pressured period with an obligation to be outer-directed and involved in the welfare of others, at the same time, such use of leisure should not be ruled out.

Even if one engages in such outer-oriented activity because of the gain that may accrue to the self, there is still room to argue that it is better to be selfless for selfish reasons than to be selfish for selfish reasons. Being selfish for selfish reasons may be less hypocritical, yet being selfless for selfish reasons is not necessarily hypocrisy, but rather the beginning of a growth process.[42] One has to start somewhere; and that is as good a place as any.

In the end, selflessness brings its own rewards almost spontaneously. Additionally, the behavior pattern is a mutually reinforcing one which brings enjoyment and pleasure to others, and thus also to the catalyst for that enjoyment and pleasure, the self. This is leisure activity, or pleasure activity, par excellence.

7

Pleasures of the Palate

WHAT IS KOSHER?

Eating is a distinct form of pleasure. Unlike other pleasures, one cannot exist without eating. One can survive without music or without art, but one cannot survive without food and drink. In this sense, eating is a potential pleasure that, at the same time, is a necessity of life.

Because eating is such a fundamental component of life, Judaism has a full measure of legislation relative to eating and drinking, as well as abundant advice. These fuse the religious imperatives that operate in eating, as in other areas of life, with the pleasure component of eating, that also is important.

The laws of eating begin with what are referred to as the dietary laws, which prescribe what animals, fowl, and fish are kosher, or fit to be eaten. Kosher is a more modern term for what the Bible refers to as *tahor*, or pure.[1] The Bible spells out general principles and specific instances regarding which of the animals, fowl, and fish are pure —eligible to be eaten—and which are impure, or *tamai*, never fit to be eaten, except in a life-threatening emergency.[2]

Within the animal kingdom, only an animal with split hooves and a ruminating stomach (one that rechews its food) is eligible for eating.[3] Within the domain of fowl, only certain birds are permitted, such as chicken and turkey; birds of prey belong to the forbidden species.[4]

In the domain of the sea, only those fish with fins and scales are considered edible according to Jewish law.[5] For fish, unlike animals and fowl, no special preparation is necessary—no ritual slaughter or letting of the blood.[6] This is, among other reasons, a matter of simple logic. A fish can be brought to the table only by taking it out of its abode, the sea. That in itself suffocates the fish, so that any further ritual preparation would be superfluous—not the case with animals or fowl.

THE MEANING OF KOSHER

The common denominator in all of the permissible types within the species is that the food to be eaten is wholesome and nutritious. Animals with a ruminating stomach rechew their food, it is better distributed within the system, and the animal is more likely to be of a domesticated and healthful sort.[7] Birds of prey have characteristics that are not congenial to the human constitution.[8] If we are what we eat, then it is better to eat from those species as close to the human in their behavior as possible.

Fish with scales and fins are likely to have a warmer interior because of the protection afforded by the scales, so that there is a more even distribution of vital matter within, and the fish is a more nutritious food.[9]

The idea conveyed is that if we are to make use of animals or fish to nourish the human being, then it is appropriate to choose those that provide decent sustenance. If a food is enjoyable, but of dubious nutritional value, then it is not worth subjecting an animal to slaughter for a questionable human benefit.

The principle to be derived from this general corpus of legislation is that pleasure is not merely acceptable, it is also desirable; yet that pleasure must be combined with a sense of responsibility toward the species. We should only eat what sustains, rather than a food that merely pleases the palate but has no decent nutritional value.

Lest we think that we are shortchanged by this discipline, in that there are so many appealing nonkosher foods, the Talmud counters that for whatever the Torah prohibited, there is a permissible alternative.[10] For example, pork and animal blood are both forbidden foods.[11] Yet there is a species of fish, the brain of which tastes exactly like pork. The blood of the animal is let out after ritual slaughter; but the liver, which is considered total blood, is permitted after being roasted.

The Talmud thus assures that there is no desire to impose an ascetic life-style through the dietary regulations. If that were the case, then alternatives for forbidden items would not be available. And the number of prohibited animals and fish would be even greater. Instead, the legislation is directed towards imposing a humane discipline upon the individual, so that the pleasures of the palate are not catered to in an inhumane, insensitive way.

Specifically with regard to food, the Talmud asserts that individuals are destined to give an accounting of all the bounty, the delicacies of this world, that were placed before them, of which they did not eat.[12] Surely this is anything but a denial notion. Judaism maintains the view that through experiencing the delicacies of the world, one gains a greater appreciation of the full scope of creation, and of the blessings that have been placed on earth by God for humankind to enjoy.

RITUAL PREPARATION

Within the animal sphere, and also among fowl, the fact that an animal is of the permitted species, namely *tahor*, still does not guarantee that it may be eaten. There is a further preparatory procedure, known as *shehitah*, or (for want of a better term) ritual slaughter, which must be performed in order for the animal to be fit, or kosher.[13] For this procedure, an exacting set of regulations are applied.

The person who performs the *shehitah*, the *shohet*, is a Rabbi or learned individual, who has received the ordination licensing him.[14] Thus the act of preparing the animal is done by a student-scholar,[15] an individual who is by definition peace-loving and intellectually oriented, rather than a callous man of the field.

The knife that is used must be absolutely free of the slightest nick on the blade surface.[16] The actual act of slaughter is a to-and-fro motion cutting the carotid arteries and the jugular veins, without the slightest hesitation in the midst of the procedure.[17] The act of *shehitah* must start from the front of the neck; side entry is absolutely forbidden.[18] If any of these conditions have not been met, the animal is unfit to be eaten; it is not kosher.

The *shehitah* regulations guarantee that the animal is subjected to the minimal pain. All the prohibitions cited —no delay in the act of cutting, or nicks on the knife, which would yank rather than cut, among others—are to avoid extending, even for a moment, the pain to which the animal is subjected. Any such extension contravenes the law and causes the animal to be prohibited as food. The same rule, of course, applies to fowl.

This legislation also speaks volumes about the discipline involved in Judaic dietary regulations. Meat can be eaten, but only when the preparation is done in as humane a fashion as possible. Insensitivity to the animal in the process of preparing it as food for humans renders that food as inedible, nonkosher, *treyfah*.

The detailed prohibitions regarding the preparation of an animal for eating, to all intents and purposes eliminate hunting as a sport. To kill an animal for no reason whatsoever is inhumane and purposeless. To kill an animal for the purpose of eating it, from the Judaic vantage point, is also purposeless, since the act of shooting an animal makes it impossible properly to prepare it ritually through *shehitah*, so that the animal is forbidden as food. The animal can be used as human sustenance only when it is treated seriously and humanely, and not when it is the object of sport. The animals eligible for eating according to Jewish law are domesticated, and need not be hunted.

EATING MEAT

More so than with other foods, there are other restrictions or guidelines concerning the frequency with which one eats meat. In the specific commandment to be joyous on the festivals, one unique form of celebrative joy for the festivals—Passover, Pentecost, and Tabernacles—is a meal including meat and wine.[19] One may conjecture that were an individual to eat meat every day, there would be no special joy in eating meat on the festival, since it is part of the everyday diet. The correlation between joy and eating meat indicates that meat, like wine, is not an everyday staple, and its specialness is what lends it a joyous quality.

There is a biblical directive that one should only eat meat when one has the appetite for it.[20] One should not eat meat perfunctorily; only when it is specifically desired. Forced or indifferent eating is not qualitative eating, and such eating is no justification to legitimize slaughtering animals.

It is clear that Judaism does not espouse strict vegetarianism, although in its guidelines concerning the eating of meat, it shows a particular sensitivity to the fate of the animal. It is recognized that since the human being is the crown of creation, everything else in the universe is there to serve the human being. However, the human being has no right to exercise dominion, but must exercise disciplined control. The pleasure of eating meat is an acceptable pleasure, but only if it is not a privilege which is abused.

How to Eat

General guidelines concerning eating inculcate a fundamental respect for food as a gift of God, to be respected, not thrown about, or gulped. A person who eats food that is unfit has transgressed in a threefold way: first, by eating unfit food the person has degraded the self; secondly, he has degraded the food; thirdly, he has uttered a blessing for no reason and has thus evoked God's name in vain.[21] Clearly, there is a profound responsibility to eat properly and respectfully. Unfit food not only is nutritionally undesirable, but is a desecration of the food and of the body; food and the body are both gifts of God to be treated as of the utmost sanctity.

Eating itself must be done in a relaxed frame of mind. Thus, one who eats in the marketplace is comparable to a dog.[22] The individual who cannot control himself, who cannot wait to take home the food that was bought in the marketplace, to eat it in a dignified setting, behaves like a glutton, without control, and eats more like an animal than like a human being.

The individual should eat sitting down, and should carefully masticate the food before swallowing.[23] One does not find blessing in the intestines of an individual who is a glutton, who swallows the food without properly chewing it.[24] This is bad digestive practice, and also at the same time diminishes the enjoyment of eating.

If the food tastes good, chewing it more before swallowing it only adds to the enjoyment, and increases the individual's appreciation of the food. This is not only more preferable from a strictly health related point of view, but also from the point of view of the enjoyment factor.

The leisurely atmosphere and relaxed feeling at eating should also carry over to the period following. In the words of the Talmud, a person who eats and gets up immediately or who drinks and gets up immediately is among those who are closer to death than to life.[25] Aside from the medical implications, one can read in this a charge that individuals should not eat with one foot out the door, and by so doing compromise their appreciation of the food and the efficiency of the digestive process. One who eats with one foot out the door does not concentrate on the food. Instead, one has other thoughts in mind when eating, and thus does not properly stimulate the digestive enzymes, does not eat properly, does not value the food as it should be valued, misses out on a basic component of life, and is further removed from life.

How Much to Eat

A number of illuminating insights on overeating are presented in rabbinic writings. One is the interesting statement that from a meal from which you derive much pleasure, you should push your hands away.[26] That is, you should enjoy your meal; but if you enjoy it too much, there is a good possibility you may overdo. If that occurs, then all that you gain is a temporary pleasurable experience, soon to be negated by the harmful aftereffects. The only "gain" in eating too much is that "One who increases in eating will increase what is released."[27] Thus there is no value gained from overeating; in fact, it is a waste.

This recalls the pithy expression in the Talmud, previously referred to, to the effect that one is wealthy who has a privy close by to the dining table.[28] This not only speaks of the shortage of private privies in previous generations but also of the awareness by a wise (therefore wealthy) person of how much of the food will go to sustain the body, and how much would end up in the privy. With this awareness, one will eat in proper measure and enjoy immediately and ultimately what is eaten, rather than gorge oneself so that the body cannot utilize all that it has ingested.

Ultimately, more is lost through overeating than is lost through undereating. As was earlier cited, "More people have succumbed because of the pot than have succumbed because of famine."[29] With obvious limitations, what you do not eat cannot hurt you as much as what you do eat that is harmful; either because it is unfit food or because it is eaten in an unfit manner.

OTHER VARIABLES

The setting for eating is also considered important. The ideal atmosphere that is conducive to properly enjoying a meal is one in which one actually can see what one eats, with the digestive juices stimulated by the sight as well as by the smell.[30] Thus, a person should eat in the daytime, or when the food is visible.[31]

Certain foods are singled out as especially beneficial to the person, even essential: fish, for example, particularly if small and unsalted, is good for the digestion and also for bodily strength.[32] A complement of fruit and vegetables is absolutely essential, as evidenced by the regulation that one is forbidden to live in a city that does not have a good supply of fruit and vegetables.[33] Hot fruits are advised in winter, and cold fruits in summer,[34] each of course balancing out with the weather conditions to maintain an equilibrium within the body.

The breakfast meal is singled out as being of special importance.[35] An interesting comment relative to this is that before eating in the morning, one has two hearts, but after eating, only one heart.[36] If we take the heart to be the seat of intelligence and emotions, this conveys that before eating one is not clear and coherent, and is muddled in judgment. But after sustenance, the individual has "only one heart"; then he can concentrate, has focus and orientation, and can get on systematically with daily activity.

OVERINDULGENCE

Concerning overindulgence and overemphasis on meat, the Bible reports on what could be called a "meat crisis." "And the mixed multitude that was among them fell a lusting . . ."[37] The mixed multitude contended that a steady diet of manna from heaven was sickening; they wanted meat. God's response to this was that if the people wanted meat, they would get meat—not for one day but for 30 days—"until it comes out of your nostrils and it become vomit to you."[38] Why was God's response of such a nature?

One of the essential aspects of the Judaic way of life as it was evolving was that it proposed self-control for fulfillment's sake; it proposed a disciplined life in which the discipline itself is seen as the necessary quality for attaining fulfillment. There are specific times assigned for everything, so that each experience is given due attention and is thus best appreciated. It was the element of control that was manifestly projected in the disciplined supply of food by way of the manna. Rebellion against this was tantamount to a rebellion against the entire way of life that was being developed for the Israelites. The rebels rejected control and instead demanded a life of instant gratification.

God reacted by attacking the very philosophy of the rebels. Meat is good, no doubt. But a surfeit is sickening. Thereby the people will be taught a lesson. They will be made to realize that even the choicest, and lustful things in life become ordinary and even distasteful in overabundance or overindulgence. There is a time and a place for every experience, but too much indulgence destroys the very beauty of any experience.

Midrashic commentary equates "very good" with death. What is *good* is equated with life; but what is *very* good is equated with death.[39] This echoes, in effect, the major point of the "meat crisis"; that too much of anything kills life, and the beauty of any experience is enhanced by the special quality with which it is invested.

Blessing Before

Perhaps the most all-encompassing of the regulations for eating is the standard obligation to recite a specific blessing before beginning to eat,[40] and another on concluding a meal, or even a snack.[41] The Talmud, in seeking to reconcile differing verses, one of which ascribes ownership of the earth to God,[42] and the other, which declares that the heavens are God's, but the earth God has given to mankind,[43] suggests that the one verse applies "prior to the recitation of a blessing," and the other, "subsequent to the recitation of a blessing."[44]

That is, if an individual eats before acknowledging God as the source of the food, then he is literally stealing from God through the failure to acknowledge that it is taken from God. However, through the recitation of a blessing, with its concomitant acknowledgment and appreciation of God as the source, God grants title of the food to the individual.

A blessing, properly enunciated, establishes a mood of gratitude and appreciation for everything that one eats or drinks. In such an appreciative mood, one is less likely to be gluttonous, since one realizes the source as outside oneself. One is likely to be more careful with a precious gift.

We sing God's praises before eating, and then engage in the eating, which itself can and ideally should be in the context of an affirmation of God. Eating can be a religious experience, and is certainly more open to the religious dimension than is abstinence and fasting. The Nazarite who vows to abstain merely from wine is considered a sinner.[45] One who would abstain from more than just wine, who would deprive the self of all the nourishment that God has made available, is obviously an even greater sinner.[46]

BLESSING AFTER

At the conclusion of the meal, another blessing or series of blessings is recited, again giving thanks to God for all that God has done to sustain the person.[47] It is logical that if one blesses God even before having appreciated the benefits of nourishment, one should also express such thanks after one is satisfied.[48] Satisfaction does not mean satiety; it is rather a sense of contentment for having received enough sustenance to go on with meaningful and vigorous activity. One can eat to feed the body, and one can also eat to revitalize the soul. The nourishment of the soul, in which one eats in proper measure, is the highest form of satisfaction, a transmutation of eating into a true physical and spiritual pleasure.[49]

There is a lesson in the obligation to give thanks when satisfied, in addition to giving thanks when in need. It is the habit of too many, that when they need something from others, they are very compliant and ingratiating, but once the request has been granted, they take it as their rightful share. There may be a token thanks, but not the profound appreciation that cements a lasting relationship. With regard to meals, the habit is established of always thanking before and after, of expressing gratitude even when one is perfectly satisfied. We learn the unbounded nature of appreciation, the rightfulness of constant thankfulness to God for all the good that has been placed in the world.

The pleasure of eating, like other pleasures, is thus placed into a specific context with a distinct focus. Eat, drink, and enjoy fully the pleasures of the palate as indeed has been desired by God. Obviously, if human beings have to eat in order to remain alive, it would be folly for us to find eating a distasteful experience. Since eating is identified with life itself, eating as an unpleasurable experience would commensurately color all of life as distasteful. On the other hand, if food is delicious and inviting, then precisely because it is a basic component of life it transfers these qualities to all of life. Thus eating is a paradigm of life itself.

THE PURPOSE

Finally, there arises the almost hypothetical question of whether one eats to live, or lives to eat. The ideal, of course, would be that one eats in order to live meaningfully. When one lives to eat, one makes eating an end in itself, a situation that is problematic with eating and with other forms of pleasure experience. Not only is it philosophically undesirable, it is also functionally less fulfilling, because to experience any pleasure in a consuming, gluttonous manner robs that pleasure of its highest value.

The idea of eating in order to live is perhaps best expressed in the statement: "three who have eaten at a table and who have spoken there words of Torah, it is as if they had eaten at the table of the Omnipresent";[50] it is as if God was one of the table partners.

"Three who eat together" conveys a special intent to enjoy one another's company; it is more than just eating perfunctorily in order to get on with other things. It establishes a *presence*; and therefore is set as the minimum for the description of what one does at that meal—or what three do.

The basis for the statement that three who eat and study God's word are as if God is present is the verse, "and He said to me; 'this is the table that is before the Lord.' "[51] This is the last part of a verse; the first deals with the measurements of the altar in the Temple to be built by God, and shown in a vision to the prophet Ezekiel. Ezekiel did not see a table in this vision; he was shown an altar. After having been shown the altar, its measurements, and the substance from which it would be made, Ezekiel says, "and He said to me; 'this is the table that is before the Lord.' "[52] In other words, the table conforms to the measurements of the altar; but it is *before* God, even after the destruction of the Temple.

Unlike the altar itself, which is nonexistent in exile, the table itself is existent. The table is the altar in the era subsequent to the destruction of the Temple. Since there are no sacrifices after the destruction of the Temple, it must be that this table is for those who eat, but who eat in a Godly atmosphere; they share God's words at the table. This then becomes God's table, or the surrogate altar in the era of exile.

This eating, in a Godly context, is a truly spiritual experience, one which imbues a creature pleasure with covenantal significance.

8

Sensual Pleasure

Unique Experiences

The pleasure of male and female united in love is a most unique pleasure experience. In its ultimate manifestation, it is a pleasure which is indescribable, a heavenly bliss not comparable to other pleasures. But it is a distinct form of pleasure that takes two. It takes two separate individuals, who are involved together in the pursuit, to experience sensual pleasure.

When one forces the self upon the other, usually the male upon the female, the experience is the reverse of pleasurable; it is closer to rape, and is painful and traumatic. The rapist may feel a temporary sense of release; but there is no love, there are no shared feelings. Rape remains an act of violence which is a distortion of everything that is human.

Sensual pleasure demands the full cooperation of the two individuals involved. Anything less than full cooperation proportionately limits the pleasure that can be experienced. Depending upon the degree to which one forces oneself on the other, this type of imposition of the self on another may not legally be considered rape, but certainly is morally a form of rape.

Sensual pleasure is unlike other pleasures in two main respects. First, as has been pointed out, for sensual pleasure to approach ultimate bliss it takes the cooperation of the two involved, unlike artistic and musical pleasures, or the pleasures of the palate, which can be experienced by the individual alone.

Secondly, the sensual experience, if improperly approached, can be very painful, physically and emotionally, for either or both of the individuals. There is thus an implicit challenge in the sensual experience, to each of the partners, to approach the situation properly, and to thus assure that it is a pleasurable rather than a painful event.

DEVIATING EXPERIENCES

With all the emphasis on the sensual experience being that of male and female together, one is surely likely to wonder about contrary types of pleasure experiences which seem to find their way into modern manuals on sensual expression.

Two specific exceptions to the rule that sensual pleasure evolves from the union of male and female are: 1) the homosexual and lesbian relationship; and 2) masturbation, or self-induced orgasm. The one deals with the sensual experience of two, but they are of the same sex; the other deals with a sensual experience which is self-induced and is done on one's own. What is the Judaic attitude to these forms of sensual expression?

The physical union of male and female relates back to original cration. Adam, the first human, was, according to Talmudic tradition, a combination of male and female,[1] and the surgery performed on Adam was not the building of a female from a spare rib. The surgery, instead, was more analogous to a Siamese section, which separated the male and female components. When male and female unite and literally become as one, they reenact or recreate the oneness that prevailed when the original human being was placed on this earth. The male-female union is the paradigm of oneness; it is the natural way.

The Bible speaks in clear, uncompromising terms about the practice of homosexuality, condemning it as an abomination, a breach of capital import.[2] Lesbianism, while not in the same punitive category, is also strictly proscribed.[3] For the believing individual, the fact that a specific behavior or action is prohibited by biblical or rabbinic law is reason enough to accept and abide by the prohibition. The philosophical rationale is not necessary.

Nevertheless, some rationalization of the prohibitions that are at work is in order, specially considering the libertarian climate in contemporary society, in which some see nothing wrong with individuals doing "their own thing," as long as it does not harm others.

Parenthetically, it may be added that the recent epidemic outbreak of certain types of sexually transmitted diseases has shown that the narcissistic philosophy of "self-indulgence as long as it does not harm others" is a bankrupt philosophy.[4] It is precisely as a result of individuals doing too much of their own thing that society is now paying a terrible price.

COMMUNAL CONTEXT

At the outset, it should be stated that when Judaism prescribes norms, these are norms for the entire community, and they are geared towards enhancing that community. Any individual may claim that he is the exception, and that his own deviance will not harm the community; but the Judaic view has always been that either everyone adheres to the norms, or no one adheres.[5]

Norms do not become communal standards if it is left up to each individual to choose whether he wants to keep to them or not. The strength of Judaism throughout the ages has resided in the communal commitment to live out the norms of tradition as a community.

Therefore, it is best to approach the matters of homosexuality and lesbianism from a communal, rather than from an individual vantage point. In the communal context, if the norm were homosexuality and lesbianism, there would be no community of the future. In the absence of male-female relationships, no procreation would ensue, and humanity would die in its own self-constructed bed of narcissistic, selfishly pursued pleasure.

Homosexual and lesbian pleasure, does not give birth to future generations. It allows for individuals to enjoy themselves without taking upon themselves responsibility for educating a future generation, since they have, to all intents and purposes, given up on creating a future. Homosexuality and lesbianism are radical forms of infatuation with the present and obliviousness to the long-range.

Judaism's attitude to sensual pleasure is anything but prudish; yet it insists that such pleasure must incorporate a sense of responsibility to the partner and at the same time, toward the future. After all, the present, and those who enjoy the present, owe that reality to a past which was concerned about the future.

Since both homosexuality and lesbianism as communal norms would destroy community, they are condemned as wrong not only on a communal level, but also on an individual level. Judaism, as has been pointed out, does not make distinctions between communal norms and individual rights. What is communally wrong is wrong for the individual, and what is communally proper should become the normative behavior of the individual.

It is absurd to start thinking along the lines of, well, if only 50 percent of the population engage in homosexual or lesbian behavior, but the other 50 percent are heterosexual, the community will maintain itself, but at 51 or 52 or 60 percent, the community must intervene. Either the issue is one of biblical-rabbinic right and wrong, or it is no issue at all.

Of course, contemporary society, specially democratic society with its emphasis on individual rights, gives almost limitless license to individuals to choose their own sexual preference. This effectively prevents any legal intervention on the grounds that such preference violates biblical proscription. Nevertheless, this does not and should not stop the Jewish community from espousing the norms that have sustained it for the millennia, even at the same time that it shows appropriate understanding for individual circumstances that may have led to the choice of a deviating life-style.

SENSUALITY ALONE

As for self-induced, self-experienced pleasure, such as masturbation, this form of sensual experience is somewhat similar to the homosexual and lesbian experience in that it wastes sensual energy in a way that cannot lead to procreation, and as a life-style is certainly outside the framework of a community which seeks at least to replenish itself, and to build upon itself for a viable future.

Masturbation is generally referred to in the Talmud as "wasteful emission of seed."[6] Implicit in this terminology is that seed can be used to good advantage, and by spilling it for individual pleasure one distorts the purpose for which the seed was created.

That purpose is twofold. One, as has been pointed out, is use as the building blocks for a procreating community which extends itself into future generations. The other, more primary waste in this form of sensual expression—or release, to be more precise—is that it is achieved in the absence of a love relationship with a partner.

The seed, whether or not it carries with it the ability to procreate, and independent of whether the female of that partnership is capable, through that sexual experience, of conceiving,[7] the seed is an instrumentality for conferring love on an other. Its being reduced to focus on the self *only* is considered a heinous crime of the highest order, a moral waste of an opportunity to share and instead using that sharing opportunity selfishly.

PROHIBITED RELATIONS

Another form of sensual expression that is biblically prohibited, is that which involves male and female who are prohibited to one another either because they are closely related,[8] or because one or another of the partners is still attached by marriage to someone else.[9] The first category is that of incest, consanguineous relationships; and the other is that of adultery.

Adultery as a norm destroys the sanctity of the marital compact, and turns awry the natural process by which parentage is clearly established. In an adulterous society, the children do not know who their parents are, and fathers do not know who their children are. In the absence of a clear indication of who is responsible for whom, children may be deprived of the unconditional love and unsurpassed devotion that comes from parents clearly committed to their progeny. Adultery destroys the fabric of coherent society.

Consanguineous relationships, in which individuals are intimate with people to whom they are closely related, such as a father and daughter or a son and mother, deprive marriage of the *reaching out* quality; the extending of the self towards another, which should be one of the operative dynamics in marriage.

As Maimonides has pointed out, the prohibited relationships are those involving individuals with whom one usually grows up, and with whom there already is a built-in familiarity.[10] As such, there is no extention of the self toward another, no effort to reach out and understand an other. Instead, it is more a union of root and branch, a shriveling up into oneself, which is usually devoid of the self-transcending quality so vital to marriage.[11]

This brief excursus into the area of prohibited relationships serves as a background against which to approach the Judaic attitude to sensuality as the legitimate experience of a surpassing pleasure.

THE TWO IMPULSES

Jewish tradition divides human desires into two specific types, the one which is called *yetzer tov*, commonly defined as the positive desire, or the desire to do good, and the *yetzer harah*, which is defined, somewhat erroneously, as the evil impulse.[12] The translation of *yetzer harah* as evil impulse is inaccurate because the term *evil impulse* implies that anything which emanates from that mode of expression is evil.

It probably is more correct to look upon these two components, or impulses, as propensities, as potentialities that can be actualized in either direction. The propensity for good is self-understood, while the propensity for "bad" really is more correctly defined as the propensity to actualize one's instinctual desires. Very often the actualization of one's instinctual desires can be bad, or harmful; but it is not necessarily the case.

As a matter of fact, in the biblical charge that we are obliged to love God with all our heart,[13] we are told that this applies to loving God with both impulses, the *yetzer tov* and *yetzer harah*.[14] Obviously, if the *yetzer harah* is to be an instrumentality expressing our love of God, it could not in itself be evil. Additionally, it is asserted that this impulse not only is not evil, it is potentially important, even crucial, for were it not for this impulse, the human being would not build a house, get married, have children, or conduct business affairs.[15] Thus we are looking here not at intrinsic evil, but at a behavior expression that has the potential to turn into evil, but by the same token can be used for positive fulfillment and be instrumental even toward expressing one's love of God.

CONTROL OF IMPULSE

Judaism does not demand that the human being stifle the sensual urge. This would not only be unnatural, but as is evident from previous observations, also deprives the individual of a vehicle that is vital for getting on with the basics of life, including loving another and giving birth to a future.

Instead, the instinctual expression, with its propensity to becoming an evil, is to be subordinated and channeled in the proper direction. Thus, Who is mighty? One who conquers one's passions.[16] Conquering passions is quite different from destroying the passions, or neutralizing them. The passions, when conquered, remain; but they are captive, captive to the control of a freely willing human being who decides in which manner the passion should be expressed.

The fear that prevails in Jewish tradition is that we may allow passions to overcome the individual, to become the conquerer rather than the conquered. Passions that rule can lead the human being to destructive behavior. Passions that are controlled can be directed to useful and noble purposes, none more exalted than love and compassion.

By conquering one's instinctual desire, or impulse, one is likely to avoid a syndrome that is spelled out in the Talmud, where the instinctual desire is first like a passerby, then becomes a lodger, and finally, master of the house.[17] It should never be that, and it can never become master if it is controlled from the outset.

What differentiates the great individual from the ordinary individual? One is likely to respond to this with the proposition that the great individual does not have to fight any instinctual drives, while the ordinary individual constantly wrestles with and occasionally succumbs to such drives. The Talmud, however, has a different answer; quite the opposite.

The Talmud asserts that whoever is greater than the other, one can assume that individual's instinctual desires to also be greater.[18] The great individual is the one who realizes that there are drives working within the system; but the individual, in free will, exercises greatness to overcome, overwhelm, and conquer those desires and subordinate them. The greatness inheres in the ability to channel those selfsame desires into positive pursuits and expressions.

CONTROL AND FULFILLMENT

The idea that human impulses should be under human control is nowhere more clearly delineated and more desirable than in the sexual relations between husband and wife. Because uncontrolled sexual expression can be harmful to the unwilling partner in such a sexual relationship, it is incumbent upon both husband and wife, and more primarily upon the husband, to control desires, and to correlate those desires with the wishes and emotions of the spouse.

Should one think that by engaging in such disciplined control, one is missing out, the Talmud assures us that the sexual organ is unique in that if one saturates it with overactivity, one makes it feel hungry, whereas if it is underused, it will bring great satisfaction.[19]

Uncontrolled lust very often creates a syndrome of rising expectations, to the point that expectations are no longer realistic. This leads to all sorts of sexual frustrations, which spill over into the essential relationship of husband and wife.[20]

Here lies the paradox in pleasure. The pleasure that is sought for itself tends to be elusive, while engaging in meaningful endeavor, or committing oneself to unconditional love, brings with it a unique pleasure—but as a by-product.

Sexual compatibility is no doubt vital in marriage. In fact, in the verse, "Whoever has found a wife has found good, . . .,"[21] "good" is interpreted as referring to the compatibility of the husband and wife; more specifically, sexual compatibility.[22]

But as important as sexual compatibility may be, it is not the only, or even the primary component of a marriage; more vital is the love that exists between husband and wife. And that love must on occasion call for a type of renunciation. If the husband or wife is not well, and physically not able to engage in sexual relations, this need not, indeed should not diminish the love and affection that can be shown by each to the other. A love relationship that is contingent on sex is a very shaky relationship, and one that can easily fall apart.

In any love contingent on a *thing*, when that thing is nullified, the love disintegrates; but a love that is independent of any thing will never disintegrate.[23] This Talmudic statement is followed with classic examples of both sides of love. Unconditional love, love that is independent of anything, is manifested in the love of David and Jonathan, good friends whose relationship was purely an ideological sharing of a common vision of life, and of the specific needs of the Israelite community.

On the other hand, love that is contingent upon a "thing" is exemplified in the love of Amnon and Tamar. Amnon's love of Tamar was a sensual love, a love not for what Tamar *was*, but rather of what Tamar *had*. This was not a valuational relationship in which Amnon appreciated the goodness, the kindness, the ethics of Tamar; rather it was the love of Tamar's beauty—her physical attractiveness, an attractiveness that elicited Amnon's passionate desire for sexual expression. However, once Amnon forced himself upon Tamar and ventilated his sexual desires, his "love" quickly disintegrated and turned into hate.[24]

UNCONDITIONAL LOVE

Love needs to be unconditional for a marriage to thrive. Also, if sex is simply one of the ingredients of a marriage, and not even the primary one, then the performance pressure is greatly alleviated. The couple do not see the sexual experience as a litmus test for the viability of the marriage, but as an added bounty to what already is a good thing. There is no pressure to perform because the marriage will not rise or fall based on what happens in the bedroom. However, when the love is unconditional, it is more likely that the sexual expression will be more spontaneous and also a true reflection of the feelings and emotions that are shared between the couple.

People who have unique relationships with others approach these relationships with a unique language expression. The language of a parent to a child differs from the language of two friends. The language of business partners differs from the language of brother and sister.

By the same token, the language of husband and wife ideally differs from the ordinary language of acquaintances, or even of close friends. There is a unique language to the marital relationship that is not only verbal expression, but also a physical expression. One can therefore see the sexual relationsihp between husband and wife as the unique language of marriage.[25]

In the Judaic view, sex is not something that should be reduced to experimentation, nor should it become a gauge beforehand of whether the marriage will work or not. One can have love independent of sex, but one should not have sex that is independent of love. Where the love exists, and where its unconditionality has been firmly and legally entrenched by the marital compact, the compact to forge a life together, then sexual expression, as a physical and tangible projection of the oneness of the couple, becomes desirable. But it is a oneness having other dimensions, including a valuational oneness, and a commitment to approach life together as a team, with each seeing the self as a half needing the other in order to be a complete entity.

ACTIVE OR PASSIVE

The husband and the wife are equal partners in marriage, and they are likewise equal partners in the sexual union. It is true that biologically the sexual act seems to incline towards the man as the initiator, and the women as cooperator with the initiating male. This is true merely in biological fact, but not to the extent of designating the man as the active partner and the woman as the passive partner. Talmudic tradition is very clear about the fact that the woman is not merely a passive partner, and in many instances her active role is even greater than that of the man.

For example, the Talmud extols the Israelite women who were separated from their husbands by great distances in the time of Egyptian subjugation.[26] This was part of the Egyptian strategy of cutting off Israelite posterity by making it impossible for the husbands to have conjugal relations with their wives. The distances between the slaves and their wives were so great that it was impossible for the men ever to return home and be back in time the next day to meet their work quotas.

This, however, did not spell the end for the Israelite community, because the Israelite women took the initiative, and left their own homes to go and meet their husbands. The husbands, obviously weakened from the intense workload that was imposed upon them by the

Egyptians, were in no shape to engage in sexual union. The Israelite wives understood this, and were able, through their own unique expression of love to their husbands, to elicit from them a sexual responsiveness that allowed sexual relations to take place. Jewish survival is the history of affirming and extending life in the most difficult circumstances, and the actions of these heroic women are paradigmatic of this.

The Talmud is lavish in the praise of these Israelite women who, with determination, inner warmth, and strength, were able to achieve what under normal circumstances would have been considered out of the question.[27] This can hardly be consistent with relegating the woman to a passive role. Quite the contrary, the Talmudic statement lauds the woman's role as an active and sensitive partner in the sexual relationship.

It could hardly be otherwise than that the woman is an active partner. If the woman perceived herself as a purely passive and readily available partner, the husband would never really know whether he is synchronizing or not; he could not be sure whether he is engaging in sexual relations or sexual ventilation. It is sexual relations that is asked of the husband and the wife, not sexual ventilation of either by means of the other.

UNIQUE APPROACHES

The Talmud tells of one of the sages who offered specific advice to his daughters before they married, regarding sexual technique. That advice essentially was that the daughters should try to heighten their husband's desire through a discrete and delicate combination of physical sharing and withholding, until reaching the climactic stage.[28] Surely that sage was not suggesting passivity for his daughters; likewise neither does Jewish tradition suggest passivity in the sexual situation for the wife.

The Talmud observes that the husband indicates his desire for sexual encounter through a verbal statement, whereas the wife indicates such readiness through her heart, or through her very being.[29] Against the background of previous quotes regarding the wife's active role in the sexual relationship, this can hardly be seen as an argument for the wife's passivity.

Instead, the Talmud here observes that the husband is more likely to demand or directly ask verbally, whereas the wife will be less likely to place demands on the husband. Rather, she will be more likely tactfully to indicate her desires through her own demeanor. Obviously, neither partner functions well in the sexual relationship when forced to react to the demands of the other.

The Talmud sees the superiority of the woman's approach, that of making one's preferences manifest, but not demanding that these desires be met. It is left for the husband to apprehend, and to be sensitive to these desires; to respond accordingly in full spontaneity, and therefore without pressure to perform. This, of course, is the ideal that elevates marriage from need gratification and need satisfaction to the spontaneous expression of love fully comprehended and apprehended by each for the other. It stands to reason that this synchronized love does not evolve instantaneously, but develops naturally over the course of the years, as the feelings and attentiveness of the husband for the wife and the wife for the husband are intensified.

Discipline and Sensitivity

Regarding the discipline that needs to prevail in the sexual relationship for that component of the marriage to blossom to its full potential, nothing is more vital than the discipline of fully appreciating the mood and the desire of the other partner; and then, to the best of one's ability, to correlate with that mood, and to respond accordingly. This applies both to husband for wife, and to wife for husband.[30]

Discipline is thus reciprocal. It obviously speaks of the capacity to control oneself when one sees that one's partner is not willing or able, even though one's desires may be importunate, even difficult to control. The other side of discipline is the capacity to be more responsive to one's partner, to engage willingly in the sexual encounter, even if one's present mood is not of strong desire. This formal discipline probably demands a high degree of the capacity to transcend oneself, and to place a primacy on the situation and condition of one's partner. Clearly, this type of reaction and discipline is useful not only for the conjugal experience, but also for the totality of the marriage.

Another area of discipline in approaching the sexual encounter relates to the responsibility of the husband not to dominate in overzealous passion, and instead to arouse the feelings of his wife through honestly felt words of intimacy, expressing his genuine love of and appreciation for his wife.[31]

The husband may be ready to launch the sexual encounter, the wife may likewise be ready to enter into it; but it is vital that the husband not assume that the wife responds at the same speed, or that she is at the exact same point of arousal as he. Mood correlation, and the establishment of an intimate love setting through well chosen and honestly meant words, is therefore urgent.

An added element of discipline in approaching the sexual relationship relates to the balanced mood that both partners share when engaging in sexual communication. This balance includes the advisability of not overeating or undereating, but rather having had a moderate, balanced meal that has had enough time to digest.[32] Uncontrolled consumption of food, or deprivation, are not the preparatory steps that conduce to ideal sexual communication.

The conjugality should be approached in an atmosphere of control, precluding a situation when either or both of the partners are drunk.[33] In drunkenness, one is not aware, and one can inadvertently abuse the other verbally or physically. The sexual relationship may be a "high," but it is one that is achieved in sober reality, and in profound appreciation of the other, an attitude highly improbable, even impossible, in a drunken state.

LEGALIZED DISCIPLINE

Over and above all the recommended disciplines effective in creating the atmosphere for profound sexual expression, there is an area of discipline that is more than helpful advice. An entire corpus of legislation in Jewish law governs the sexual relationship between husband and wife. These rules, commonly referred to as *taharat hamishpahah* (purity of the family) regulations,[34] establish a cyclic pattern of union and withdrawal within the marriage, on a regular basis.

The basic component of this legislation prescribes that during the time that the woman is menstruating, and for a full 7 days subsequent to the cessation of the menstrual flow, marital relations are prohibited.

Following the conclusion of 7 complete days of no menstrual discharge, the wife is obliged to immerse in a ritual bath called a *mikvah*, after which sexual relations between husband and wife are resumed.

In effect, there is an enforced period of abstinence of at least 12 days during the course of a normal cycle of 28 days or thereabouts. Regardless of how much the husband and the wife may desire sexual expression during that period, it is prohibited by Jewish law.

This may appear to be the crude intervention of a legal code in a relationship that should be spontaneous and free from all outside intrusion. If the couple so desire, why should they not join in sexual embrace?

The intervention of Jewish law in this regard is effectively to introduce, to the marital relationship, a discipline that transcends individual feelings. One may conjecture that Jewish tradition, from biblical times onward, works on the assumption that too much of a good thing can devalue it. This was seen to be the point of God's response when the people rebelled at the diet of manna,[35] and is potentially a very serious danger in the marital sphere. The discipline imposed on the marital dynamics is intended to forestall the possibility that the sexual relationship become routinized.

DENIAL AS FULFILLMENT

It should be made patently clear that the menstrual law regulations are not conceived as an exercise in self-denial, but rather quite the reverse. The denial during the menstrual period is geared towards making the subsequent sexual encounter more meaningful. The notion that the period of sexual encounter is a prelude to the period of denial runs contrary to the Talmudic understanding of this legislation.

In the words of the Talmud, the regulations governing sexual frequency and the time intervals when sexual relations are proscribed, are in order to recreate the atmosphere of loving desire that prevailed for the couple upon their getting married.[36] The period of abstinence is designed to increase mutual fondness.

The law, by creating a period of abstinence governed by the physiological state of the wife, obviates the matter of sexual frequency becoming a bone of contention, a subject for negotiation between husband

and wife. The husband cannot blame the wife for not wanting him, since it is the law which says that she cannot; and since the wife cannot, neither can the husband.

It may also be assumed that under normal circumstances, following a prolonged physical separation—and even 12 days is "prolonged" in an intimate relationship—it will be the desire of both husband and wife to spontaneously come together in sexual embrace. The law, therefore, can be seen as establishing the structural framework in which sexual spontaneity can naturally express itself. A matter as crucial to the marriage as sexual expression, the law does not leave to chance, but creates a governing legislation to which both husband and wife must adhere.

The laws that govern the prohibited period of sexual relations are referred to as the *nidah* (menstruant) laws; those that govern the obligation to have sexual relations are called *onah* laws. The term *onah* describes the time that belongs to the wife as her legitimate right, the time that must be shared intimately with her by the husband.

THE RIGHT TIME

There are prescribed times in the marital cycle in which the husband is obliged to engage in sexual encounter with his wife. One such time, as has been pointed out, is when the menstrual period has concluded with the wife's immersion in the *mikvah* (ritual bath). The wife is assuredly refreshed and invigorated, and ready once again to resume physical contact with her husband. The husband must respond sensitively to this situation, and is not allowed to play games with his wife, whether it may be playing hard to get, or bargaining for something else by withholding sexual favors. This contravenes the law.[37]

Of course, stating that any practice is against the law does not guarantee that it will be avoided by either or both of the partners. There are too many instances when people flout the law, hide behind it, or twist it to their own purposes. In espousing the Judaic position on an issue, one must take into account that people misinterpret the legislation. This should not detract from the essence, the intent, or the wisdom of the legislation itself.

Sexual visitation is likewise obligatory on the husband when he is about to embark on a journey, or, again, upon his return.[38] This too falls into the general category of a separation of duration, at the onset or at the conclusion of which it may be anticipated that the wife's desire for sexual embrace is high.

More primarily, the essential obligation of the husband is to be sexually responsive to the wife whenever he senses her desire.[39] This is independent of the time when she concludes her menstrual cycle, or before and after separation by a journey.

In general, the frequency of sexual visitation depends upon the physical condition of both husband and wife, and more specifically, it is dependent upon the husband's capacity adequately to address the wife's sexual needs. A person who is robust would be obliged to provide more frequent sexual visitation, with the proviso that this is also the desire of the wife.[40]

At no time can the husband impose his sexual desire upon his wife.[41] The law clearly demarcates a regulatory period of sexual abstinence, but that interval revolves around the wife's physical state. When it is anticipated that the wife experiences desire, then the husband is obliged to respond.

To Please the Partner

Should one think that the husband's obligation is merely to be a sexual functionary dispensing favors to a desirous spouse, it should be made clear that this is not the case. The precise obligation of the husband is to engage in sexual encounter with his wife in such a way that after completion of the sexual experience, the wife is left in a happy and fulfilled state.[42]

The *onah*, or sexual visitation obligation, rests upon the husband. This is consistent with the pattern previously discussed, whereby the requirement to marry, and the responsibility to procreate, are the husband's obligations.[43] The woman is not placed in the position of having to marry or to endure the pain of childbirth, but she is certainly encouraged to decide free-willingly in favor of these options.

The husband is the one who is obliged to marry, and is likewise the one who has the obligation, legally speaking, to confer the pleasures of marriage upon his marital partner. This does not exempt the wife, nor does it indicate that she plays a secondary role. It merely establishes and delineates areas of legal responsibility. Both can be held accountable for failure to cooperate in the sexual component of marriage, and either has the right to divorce because of the noncompliance of the other.[44]

The emphasis, in the *onah* obligation of the husband, is placed on his responsibility to gladden his wife. This may seem a performance pressure, and may appear a difficult burden to bear.

However, it should be appreciated that Judaic tradition does not mandate the time of intromission for the husband, nor does it obligate the husband to show extraordinary sexual prowess. It obliges the husband to experience his pleasure in the context of his purposeful and intentional desire to ensure that the wife experiences pleasure as well.

The husband's self-transcending approach in the sexual relationship, in which his primary objective is to assure that the wife is gladdened by the love that she feels from her marital partner, is much more conducive to his own sexual fulfillment than is a narcissistic, me-first or me-only approach in the sexual relationship. The husband who focuses on his own thrill and is oblivious to the partner not only is more likely to abuse the partner, but is also eventually more likely himself to be less than fulfilled in the sexual relationship—devoid of love as that relationship is, and hyped up as it is by excessive expectations, which can not realistically be fulfilled.

TECHNIQUE AND MYSTIQUE

As for the sexual technique that is most likely to please the wife, it is suggested by Judaic tradition that lengthier intromission, waiting for the wife to be properly aroused before the husband begins rapid thrusting, is the most desired approach.[45] This assures the wife's readiness and likewise assures the husband's potency at the time when the wife is ready. Such a momentous meeting is likely to facilitate the climactic sensual bliss in the sexual encounter.

The husband's ejaculation prior to the wife's arousal, of course, leaves the wife frustrated, even feeling herself an object that has been used. Admittedly, the timing will not always synchronize, and either or both of the partners may not experience orgasm. This is to be expected on occasion over the duration of a marriage, but should be the exception rather than the rule. And, when sexual satisfaction falls short of anticipation, emotional compensation is always possible by prolonged caress and embrace. Such gestures assure each partner of the other's unconditional love, love independent of "successful" sex.

The sexual encounter is an experience to be savored; one preceded by intimate expressions and fond embraces, and also followed by tender closeness, a physical union that is of course enhanced by the peak pleasure just experienced.

One who separates from his spouse immediately following a sexual climax is, again, one of those considered closer to death than to life.[46] Perhaps the import here is that such an individual misses out on one of life's greatest beauties, the intimate embrace of a couple in love, and instead distorts the sexual union into a mere release of sexual energy rather than entering into a true love experience.

The Talmudic statement that the husband can do as he pleases with his wife in the sexual encounter gives the husband quite a liberal license.[47] However, against the background of the awareness that the husband must never coerce his wife, and must always assure that she desires the sexual encounter, it is obvious that this does not give the husband carte blanche.

The statement serves, more than anything else, to loosen any inhibitions of the husband in seeking to confer pleasure on his wife. On the assumption that the wife truly desires the sexual experience, the husband can then do what he feels like. That is to say, he need not feel inhibited but can be free and open in the sexual encounter. It is assumed that he can do what he feels like as long as, and only as long as he has the full agreement and cooperation of his wife.

Two interesting nuances of the sexual encounter are 1) that it should not take place in daylight,[48] and 2) as was earlier noted, that the husband should not stare at his wife's sexual organs.[49] Both of these regulations are geared toward assuring that the wife does not become a mere repository for the husband's lust. The wife is not an object to be stared at, and the sexual union is more than a mere physical experience.

In darkness, in the absence of light, the union is between two human beings rather than between two bodies. The regulations concerning darkness and avoidance of staring are thus another discipline measure invoked to assure that the full dignity and sanctity of the marital relationship is kept intact.

The sexual relationship, as has been pointed out, is unique in that it is a pleasure which takes two to fully and properly experience. The person who catches, filets, fries, and then devours fish, claiming, "I love fish," is indulging in self-deception. That person does not love the fish, which is manhandled; that person loves the self, and uses the fish in order to indulge the self.[50] Such a fish-feast approach to the sexual encounter is obviously destructive, since self-serving sexuality ignores, and by such ignoring, effectively abuses the partner.

A Pleasure Paradigm

The sexual encounter, more so than other forms of pleasure, is indeed a true paradigm for the Judaic approach to pleasure. Pleasure approached in an insensitive manner, whether it be pleasure that is experienced together or alone, can be destructive to the individual, and in a sexual experience can be destructive to others. However, the sexual encounter can be an exhilarating and meaningful expression of love, the type of pleasure that carries with it a tidal wave of positive emotion, enough to cement a relationship in everlasting affection.

When the sexual experience is approached along the lines that are suggested by Judaic tradition, with the focus on conferring pleasure upon one's wife, then the pleasure that is experienced by the husband is of a transcending quality, both physically and emotionally.[51] The Judaic law of sexual pleasure, with its strict disciplines and well-defined guidelines, offers a keen insight into how sexual pleasure is best experienced. Such an approach can well hold its own against the narcissistic tide that is overwhelming contemporary society.

The Talmud relates the fascinating story of a student who hid under the bed in his Rabbi's conjugal chamber. He was closely attentive as his Rabbi made amorous approaches to his wife that evening, and muttered to himself over the passionate behavior of his Rabbi, which obviously surprised him. The astonished Rabbi, in amazement rather than anger, asked his student what he was doing there. The student replied, "It is Torah (Jewish Law), and I need to learn!"[52]

The student's rationale was that the way one approaches one's wife in the sexual encounter is Torah, or Jewish tradition. If the student is obliged to glean from his Rabbi all that is basic in Jewish tradition, certainly the conjugal experience is included in that category.

In fact, conjugal relations is Torah, and conjugal relations at their best is Torah at its best; the most profound expression of the fundamentals of Torah, or Jewish tradition.

Life is sacred; the generating of life, both in quality and in quantity, is likewise sacred. Translated, this means that the sexual relationship, linked as it is to the qualitative and quantitative dimensions of life, is a sacred experience. We dare not profane it, or diminish its pleasurable and hence sacred essence, through ignorance or through selfishness.

9

Conclusion

The discourse on pleasure comprising this volume has covered the vast gamut of life's contingencies, including health preservation, pain, depression, eating, drinking, leisure, and sexual expression.

More than sufficient evidence from the primary sources—biblical and Talmudic statements, has been presented to indicate conclusively that classical Jewish tradition espouses a distinctly affirmative attitude to pleasure.

That affirmative attitude, however, should not be misconstrued as unbridled license to indulge in pleasure. Pleasure is part of a more all-encompassing mosaic; a necessary *component* of a meaningful life.

In the Judaic framework, the experience of pleasure unfolds within the context of faith. Belief in God is the primary affirmation. That belief concept incorporates a vision of God and of God's creations. God created the world and its inhabitants, who were placed on this earth for a purpose.

We may not know the precise purpose for which humankind was placed on this earth, yet at the same time we remain convinced that there is a purpose.

Additionally, whatever the ultimate purpose, there are more immediate meanings to be actualized. These meanings form a chain linking in the direction of the ultimate.

Clearly, the melancholy spirit is not conducive to the affirmation of God and of life. Unhappiness at being in the world is effectively unhappiness with God—the Placer—as well as with the place—the world.

Faith affirmation is closely linked with appreciation to God for granting life, and appreciation of the world in which that life unfolds. The one who appreciates is gratified, satisfied, happy, and generally eager to involve the self in meaningful activity.

Pleasure, within the Judaic framework, is not an end in itself; it is a means to an end. Pleasure is the joyful experience which makes one feel happy; pleasure is basic to creating the proper mood for meaningful endeavor. The pleasure experience itself becomes a religious act, whether it be intellectual, digestive, or sensual pleasure.

Because pleasure is so essential to faith affirmation, Judaism incorporates the experiencing of pleasure into its legal framework. The proper experiencing of pleasure is carefully nurtured, mainly through the discipline of Jewish life.

There are times to enjoy, and times to abstain. There are times to indulge, and times to refrain. The tradition itself establishes the guidelines and the appropriate mood. Judaism refuses to leave to individual whim the matter of when to engage in pleasurable activity. The matter is too serious, the possible repercussions too dangerous. The life of meaningful pleasure requires discipline.

The discipline imposed directs itself to three main components in the pleasure sphere; 1) the individual, 2) the partner, and 3) the community.

The individual is permitted an unending array of pleasures, as well as limitations restricting when and how these pleasures may be tasted. The person is required to maintain control, and not to abuse the self in the rush to indulge. The individual is called upon to sanctify the self with that which is permissible. Whatever is permissible should be approached with delicate appreciativeness.

It is understood that people generally desire self-satisfaction; but that is best achieved in moderation and in balance—the balance echoed in Hillel's famous statement; "If I am not for me, who will be for me?

But if I am for my own self only, what am I?"[1] One must balance the concern for self-satisfaction with awareness of the needs of others.

The need for balance is best illustrated in the area of sexual pleasure, pleasure that is most effectively achieved through the correlation of moods by husband and wife. When mood correlation is replaced by the unilateral imposition of desire, then one person's pleasure becomes the other person's pain.

The legally entrenched parameters for engaging in sexual pleasure have ramifications far beyond the bedroom of the home, far beyond even the home itself. It is not farfetched to suggest that the marital discipline has become embedded in the Jewish psyche. The Jew was long ago trained to tolerate delay, and to defer pleasure to a future moment. The husband or wife were conditioned to wait patiently for when the other was able.

Thus, when the enjoyments of life—the joys of marital bliss, raising children, and seeing those children mature into responsible adults—when these enjoyments were denied to them by cruel and oppressive regimes, the Jewish people were able to persevere.[2] They persevered in part because they were acclimatized to deferring pleasure, and in part because they retained faith in God and hope for a better tomorrow.

Relative to community, Judaism strives to create a deep sensitivity within the individual. Personal discipline has helped the community as a whole to overcome the perpetual threats to its existence. The community is the larger framework within which individual expression evolves. The individual is an entity unto the self, but not only unto the self. The individual is also a component of the community.

Thus, the individual is asked to refrain from sexual relations in times of famine.[3] If the community is struggling, it is not right that any person within the community behave as if nothing is wrong. Instead, everyone should commiserate with the congregation, and should feel the plight of the community as a personal pain.[4]

Failure to link with the community, and instead to enjoy life in a hermetically sealed environment of narcissistic delight, is deemed a trangression.

The training for communal sensitivity comes early in adult life. The marriage ceremony culminates with the breaking of a glass, reminding the couple of the shattering experiences of the past.[5] A wedding is a joyous event; but the ecstasy of the moment is interrupted by a dose of reality, the reality of shattered pieces, past and present. The joy of the couple is combined with serious awareness of the trials and tribulations endured by their ancestors in the past. The couple are asked to incorporate this awarenesss of the past into their vision of the future. They should be happy together, but seriously, not deliriously happy. In joy, they should find themselves and their responsibility, rather than losing themselves and their roots.

This concept of integration, integrating joy and seriousness, extends to other unavoidable realities of life. Pain and sorrow are inescapable, and these too must be confronted directly in a well integrated life. If we love, then we will have pain and sorrow when loved ones die, or go through agonizing times. An individual who has lived a long life without mourning has not really formed true human relationships.

We eat even though we know that we will eventually become hungry again. We enjoy a pleasurable experience even though we know that the experience will end, and life will return to normal. We embrace others, even though we are aware that the pain of loss is proportional to the intensity of the embrace. Love and loss are parts of a whole. The pain of loss reflects positively on the profound love. There is a time to mourn, and a time to dance.[6]

Faith in life's meaning should not be compromised by the downslope realitites. The Jew is obliged to affirm faith by the recitation of the *Shema* (faith affirmation) prayer both by day and by night.[7] The monotheistic faith in God, one God, is at once an integrated faith. Monotheism rejects the notion of heavenly subdivisions, a god of good and a god of evil, a god of day and a god of night. There is one God, and all of life relates to God. Pain and comfort, joy and sorrow, satisfaction and deprivation, are opposites that must be integrated into life if life is to have meaning, and if it is to yield meaningful pleasure.

Adam and Eve enjoyed a blissful life in the Garden of Eden. The weather was perfect, the demands minimal, the responsibility negligible.[8] Still, they deviated from prescription and were "deprived" of all their advantages. Now, they would have to work in order to eat. Bread would come by the sweat of their brow,[9] the earth's yield was held back for their sake.[10] Childbirth would become associated with pain.[11] All this was less a punishment than an adjustment to the human condition. The person who works hard to achieve has a greater appreciation of the achievement. One who eats from his own labor is praiseworthy.[12] If everything falls into one's lap without work, the person becomes spoiled, and detached.

It is not by accident, then, that the bliss of childbirth is the culmination of intense pain. The ability to work hard, the capacity to endure pain, are required if we are to experience the joys and fulfillments of life.

It was God's desire to bestow merit upon Israel, therefore God proliferated for Israel Torah to study and commandments to fulfill.[13] The Torah, studied and actualized, is a lifelong endeavor. New insights, new challenges, new fulfillments, are continually beckoning. The opportunities are endless, the satisfactions pleasant and pleasing.

The entire corpus of tradition is deemed *pleasing*. The code of law was given not to satisfy God: it was given to satisfy humankind, to elicit from humankind the full potential for kindness, empathy, warmth, and decency. Faith in God includes the trust that God, who created humankind, is in the best position to know what is good for humankind. For Jews and Judaism, "what is good" is God's formula for life, the Torah.

The confidence that the community will realize the immediate and ultimate value of Torah is reflected in the choice that is offered to the community. The people are told that they have two options before them, "life and the good" or "death and the bad."[14] Torah, of course, is equated with life and the good; rejection of Torah is identified with death and the bad.

The people are urged to *choose* life.[15] They are not ordered; they are urged to *choose*. The fact that such a critical matter was left to choice reflects the confidence that Torah is such an obviously superior option, there is little doubt what the choice would be.

And, the people are asked to choose *life*. Given that the affirmative option was for "life and the good," why not ask the people to choose the *good*? Why not make a moral choice for good over bad?

This very choice of *life* projects the primacy of life as the point of focus. *Good* is that which emanates from a meaningful affirmation of *life*. All that feeds into, and enhances life in the profound sense, is good.

The choice of life is a choice that embraces life in its totality. That embrace certainly includes the joys and the pleasures, the fulfillments and the satisfactions. But the focus is not on the pleasure; the focus is on the meaning. The pleasure ensues on its own.

The Jewish Pleasure Principle, in essence, may read as this: Enjoy life, find and give meaning to all aspects and conditions of life in accordance with the life-affirming guidelines of the Torah, and you will experience the feeling of being "*pleased*."

This is, at once, the pleasure *principle* as well as its high-yield *interest*.

Notes

INTRODUCTION

1. See Maimonides, *Mishnah Torah*, Laws of Opinions, Chapters 1 and 2.
2. Maimonides, *ibid.*, argues quite forcibly against adopting extreme habits. The notion of moderation will be developed throughout this volume.

CHAPTER 1: THE CONTEXT

1. See the incisive work by Lawrence Schiffman, *Who Was a Jew? Rabbinic and Halakhic Perspectives on the Jewish-Christian Schism* (Hoboken, New Jersey: Ktav Publishing House, 1985), in which the author explores what specifically precipitated the final break between Judaism and Christianity.
2. A clear delineation of the distinctions between Judaism and Christianity is found in the short but pointed volume of Trude-Weiss Rosmarin, *Judaism and Christianity: The Differences* (New York: Jonathan David, 1943).
3. This notion was more prevalent in the earlier stages than it is now. It should also be noted that the issue of this world's delights relative to fu-

ture bliss is a definite theme in Jewish tradition. For example, Rabbe states that "Whoever accepts for the self the pleasures of this world will be denied the pleasures of the world-to-come, but whoever does not accept the pleasures of this world shall be granted the pleasures of the world-to-come" (Avot D'Rabbe Natan, 28:5). In other places the implication is that it is best to be blessed with plenty in both worlds (Talmud, Berakhot 5b; Horayot 10b). The author of the statement cited was himself a wealthy person (Talmud, Baba Mezia 85a). Ultimate reward finds its expression in the sources. "Today to do them, and on the morrow to gain recompense" (Deuteronomy 7:11; Talmud, Eruvin 22a) links this-world righteousness with future-world reward. "Longevity, posterity, and prosperity are less matters of merit, and more matters of destiny" (Talmud, Moed Katan 28a) is a statement which seemingly detaches this world prosperity from future world reality. However prosperous one is in this world, what happens in the future depends more on one's righteousness. Wealth here does not dictate poverty there. Rabbe's statement, then, as implied in the words *accepts for the self*, seems to relate to a self-indulgent life ethos. One whose focus is on pleasure is likely to be spiritually deficient. One who is oblivious to pleasure is more likely to orient around purposeful, meaningful life. The meaning orientation definitely affects one's ultimate destiny. There are numerous biblical statements linking communal welfare to communal actualization of responsibility (for example, Exodus, 15:26; Deuteronomy 11:13–17). Good health and prosperity are thus clearly established as eminently desirable.

4. See Exodus, 18:2, and Mekhilta, which cites one view that Moses divorced his wife before returning to Egypt to assure the redemption of the Israelite community.

5. Talmud, Yevamot 63b.

6. Jerusalem Talmud, Kiddushin 4:12. *Korban HaEidah* explains that the individual who denies the self sins against the self by subjection to unnecessary affliction. The Talmud further reports on an individual who took this statement quite seriously and saved up so that during the course of the year he would have one taste of all of the new products that appeared.

7. Talmud, Taanit 11a. An alternate view in the Talmud considers one who fasts as a holy individual. R. Yosef Karo, in *Shulhan Arukh*, Orah Hayyim 571:1, basing himself on the Talmud (Taanit 11a-b), states that one who fasts, even though unable to fast without inflicting damage on the self, is considered a sinner, while one who is capable of fasting without physical harm and then fasts, is considered holy. R. Yisrael Meir Ha-Kohen, in *Mishnah Brurah*, 571:2, cites a view that an individual who feels the need to fast in order to purge the self of iniquity, is better off with

a fast that is manifested in abstention from speaking, rather than abstention from eating. By abstaining from talking, there is no damage inflicted upon the individual.

8. Genesis, 1:28;9:7. More concerning this commandment is found in Chapter 3 of this volume.

9. The age of responsibility for a male is completion of thirteen years and entering the fourteenth; for the girl, it is completion of twelve years and entering the thirteenth. See, for example, R. Yosef Karo, *Shulhan Arukh*, Orah Hayyim, 616:2.

10. Deuteronomy, 26:1–11.

11. The well-known fast days in the Jewish calendar, such as the Day of Atonement and the 9th of Av, are good examples of such limitation. Additionally, there are the more personal restrictions that apply to individuals who are in the midst of mourning. A further example, more along the line of commiserating with the community, is the Talmudic statement that an individual is not allowed to engage in marital relations in a time of famine. The individual has an obligation to share in the difficulties experienced by the community (Talmud, Taanit 11a). Tosafot on this Talmudic statement suggests that this is not an absolute law, and more a matter of optional piety.

12. Maimonides, in his *Guide for the Perplexed* (3:32), develops the notion that sacrifices were instituted within the Israelite community because the people had already become acclimatized to such mode of expression and abolishing it entirely would have been impossible. It would have backfired. Sacrifice was therefore introduced, but in a more exalted fashion, as a means of serving God. Nahmanides vehemently rejects the rationale offered by Maimonides (Leviticus, 1:9). See further Reuven P. Bulka, "The Rationale for Sacrifice: A Postscript on Abravanel's Defence of Maimonides," in *Niv Hamidrishia*, 1985, *18–19*, 41–47.

13. This idea is developed by Samson Raphael Hirsch, in his commentary to Leviticus, 1:2.

14. Leviticus, 1:2;1:14.

15. For example, Isaiah, 58:5–7: "Should such be the fast that I have chosen? Which should be a day on which a man should consider himself in a state of poverty? Is it just that he should bow down his head like a reed and envelop himself in sackcloth and ashes? Would you call this a fast and acceptable day, dedicated to God?

"Is not this rather the fast that I choose: loosening the bonds of wickedness, undoing the bands of the yoke, sending the suppressed into freedom, and every yoke shall you burst open!

"Is it not that you should break your bread to the hungry and bring the poor that are cast out into your house, when you see the naked that you cover him, and as it were of your own flesh you do not withdraw yourself from him?"

16. See Talmud, Berakhot 26b.

17. The comment found in many of the codes on adapting a more stringent posture is, "The stringent one, a blessing should be on that one." It is instructive that the terminology is not, "One who desires to be stringent, can be stringent." Instead, the statement is that the one who chooses to be stringent should be blessed in the process. This may refer to the original stringency, involving Adam and Eve, when the specific command of God not to eat from the fruit of a certain tree was extended with the added stringency of also not touching it (Genesis, 3:3). That stringency resulted in the very reverse of a blessing; hence the wish expressed that whatever stringency is adopted be for blessing. See also Talmud, Sanhedrin 29a.

18. These are essentials not only on Yom Kippur, but on any fast, as indicated in Talmud, Taanit 16a. See further Reuven P. Bulka, "The Role of the Individual in Jewish Law," in *Tradition: A Journal of Orthodox Jewish Thought*, Spring/Summer 1973, *13:4–14:1*, 124–136. The Talmud (Nazir 23b) states that "A transgression performed with good intention is as good as a precept performed for an ulterior motive." Rashi indicates that the terminology "transgression with good intention" refers to a transgression that is done for a mitzvah (fulfillment) purpose.

19. The regulation that forbids the wearing of leather shoes on the Day of Atonement is related to the obligation to feel the hardness of the earth and to feel that one is barefoot, therefore being reminded of the importance of the fast, as per Maimonides, *Mishnah Torah*, Laws of Cessation on the Tenth, 3:7.

20. Talmud, Gittin 56a.

21. Talmud, Berakhot 32b. See further the very useful volume by Aryeh Kaplan, *Jewish Meditation: A Practical Guide* (New York: Schocken Books, 1985).

22. See Eliezer Berkovits, *Faith After the Holocaust* (New York: Ktav Publishing House, 1973), especially the Introduction.

23. See Irving Rosenbaum, *The Holocaust and Halakhah* (New York: Ktav Publishing House, 1976), pp.105–108.

CHAPTER 2: THE PURSUIT OF HEALTH

1. In line with the directive that we should "Serve God in joy . . ." (Psalms, 100:2).

2. The Talmud, Shabbat 30b, asserts that the Divine Presence does not reside in a spirit of melancholy, but rather in the joy that is associated with fulfilling God's precepts.

3. Deuteronomy, 4:15.

4. See J. David Bleich, "A Survey of Recent Halakhic Periodical Literature: Smoking on Yom Tov," in *Tradition: A Journal of Orthodox Jewish Thought*, Summer 1983, *21:2*, 167–172.

5. For more on this subject, see Reuven P. Bulka, "Ethical Issues In Smoking," *Hadarom*, Nisan 1979, *48*, 53–55. (Hebrew). Also Bleich, *op. cit.*, 172–177.

6. A good general discussion of the issue is the article by Fred Rosner, "Cigarette Smoking and Jewish Law," *Journal of Halacha and Contemporary Society*, Fall 1982, *4*, 33–45.

7. See, for example, R. Aharon of Barcelona, *Sefer HaHinukh*, no. 154.

8. Even in such a commandment as the prohibition of coveting (Exodus, 20:14), Mekhilta states clearly that no punishment accrues for coveting unless and until the coveting is followed by an action.

9. See Maimonides, *Mishnah Torah*, Laws of Opinions, 4:8, 20, 21.

10. Talmud, Hullin 10a. See R. David HaLevi, *Turei Zahav* to *Shulhan Arukh*, Yore Deah, 116:2; also, R. Abraham Zvi Hirsch Eisenstat, *Pit'hay Tshuvah, ad. loc.*, 116:3.

11. Talmud, Taanit 22b, based on Genesis, 2:7.

12. Deuteronomy, 7:15.

13. Midrash Rabbah, Leviticus, 16:8.

14. Tanna D'bay Eliyahu Zuta, 3.

15. See further on this, Reuven P. Bulka, "A Theology of Pollution," in Joseph Singer (Ed.), *The Rabbinical Council Sermon Manual* (New York: Rabbinical Council Press, 1971), pp. 369–370. See, for example, 26:3–46.

16. Talmud, Tamid 32a. Rashi sees in this dialectic a reference to humility and haughtiness. However, *Maharshah* of R. Shmuel Edels posits that this dialectic concerns eating. The issue here is overindulgence rather than enjoyment in moderation.

17. Jerusalem Talmud, Terumot 8:3.

18. Jerusalem Talmud, Shabbat 14:3.

19. Avot D'Rabbe Natan, 29:6.

20. Talmud, Shabbat 153a recounts the anecdote of a sage telling his students that they should repent one day before their death. The students expressed amazement at this statement, questioning whether the individual actually knows when death will occur. To this the teacher replied, "How much

more so should the individual repent today for fear that death may come tomorrow, and thus one's entire life is spent in repentance."

21. See Exodus, 33:16; also, Talmud, Berakhot 7a, and the suggested approach to this problem in Reuven P. Bulka, *As a Tree by the Waters —Pirkey Avoth: Psychological and Philosophical Insights* (New York: Feldheim Publishers, 1980), commentary to 4:19, pp. 165–166.

22. Talmud, Gittin 69b.

23. Talmud, Shabbat, 41a.

24. See, on this subject, the excellent volume by Moshe Perlman, *Midrash HaRefuah* (Tel-Aviv: Dvir, 1926), part 1, p. 47, Note 76 in text.

25. *ibid.*, Note 76.

26. Talmud, Gittin 70a.

27. Avot D'Rabbe Natan, 26:5.

28. Talmud, Avodah Zarah 12b. See also R. Yosef Karo, *Shulhan Arukh*, Yore Deah, 116 and Hoshen Mishpat, 427.

29. Talmud, Hullin 105b.

30. See R. Yosef Karo, *Shulhan Arukh*, Orah Hayyim, 181:10, and R. Yisrael Meir HaKohen, *Mishnah Brurah*, Note 22.

31. Talmud, Shabbat 33a.

32. Talmud, Shabbat 25b.

33. See, on this subject, the commentary on R. Shmuel Edels, Maharshah.

34. Talmud, Shabbat 41a.

35. Talmud, Shabbat 82a.

36. Talmud, Berakhot 54b.

37. Talmud, Shabbat 82a.

38. *ibid.*

39. *ibid.*

40. Leviticus 20:25; Talmud, Makkot 16b.

41. Talmud, Gittin 70a.

42. Talmud, Sanhedrin 17b.

43. See, on this subject, the commentary of R. Yaakov Reisher, *Iyun Yaakov*, who suggests that the requirement to live in a city with a privy applies specifically to the Talmudic scholar, who because of intense study is generally weak. However, it is difficult to sustain this argument, since among the features required for the city is a synagogue. Certainly, the Talmud would not restrict itself in advising who should be in proximity to a synagogue, so that the statement about the requisites for living in the city would seem to apply to everyone; anyone may consider the self as a Talmud scholar for this purpose.

44. Maimonides, *Mishnah Torah*, Laws of Opinions, 4:4.

45. Talmud, Avot 3:14.

46. Talmud, Gittin 70a.
47. Talmud, Yevamot 102b.
48. As per Talmud, Shabbat 118a; Taanit 22b.
49. Avot D'Rabbe Natan, 41:4.
50. *ibid.*: "nothing compares with it."
51. See Moshe Perlman, *Midrash HaRefuah* (Tel Aviv: Dvir, 1926), part 1, p. 124, Note 35.
52. See Maimonides, *Mishnah Torah*, Laws of Opinions, 1:4. Here, Maimonides suggests a balance. One should not be easily provoked to anger, yet one should not be so dead as to have no feelings, to be so bereft of feelings that no matter what happens one never becomes angry.
53. Talmud, Taanit 20b.
54. Talmud, Avot 4:28.
55. Talmud, Berakhot 58b.
56. Midrash Rabbah, Genesis, 14:11.
57. Talmud, Nedarim 40a.
58. Tosefta, Baba Batra 1:7.
59. Jerusalem Talmud, Taanit 3:6.
60. Tanna D'Bay Eliyahu Zuta, 3.
61. Talmud, Ketuvot 111a.

CHAPTER 3: AVOIDING PAIN

1. See the dialectic in Talmud, Taanit, 11a-b; also, Jerusalem Talmud, Nedarim 9:1. See, in this title, Chapter 1, section on "Judaism on Denial," and especially footnote 7. It should be stated that this volume does not seek to make a judgment on which of the traditions is the correct one. However, the dialectic in the Talmud offers the possibility of differing approaches, and this volume merely suggests a formulation of an attitude to pleasure that is fully consistent with Jewish tradition.
2. Talmud, Avot 1:10.
3. Avot D'Rabbe Natan, 41:4.
4. Talmud, Gittin 70a.
5. See on this, Midrash Rabbah, Lamentations, 1:45.
6. Talmud, Ketuvot 59b.
7. Avot D'Rabbe Natan, 11:1.
8. See Talmud, Sanhedrin 106a, that the term *Vayeshev*, denoting dwelling in a serene environment, always is a language of pain. Perhaps this is a suggestion that when an individual desires to sit in a tranquil, worry-free environment, inevitably something happens to disturb that tranquility.

Perhaps even the excessive focus on tranquility is what leads to its interruption. The excessive attention to external stimuli actually makes one more aware of the stimuli.

9. Viktor E. Frankl, *The Doctor and the Soul: From Psychotherapy to Logotherapy* (New York: Bantam Books, 1967), p. 89.
10. Leviticus, 23:26–32. See Talmud, Yoma 74b.
11. See R. Yosef Karo, *Shulhan Arukh*, Orah Hayyim, 549, 550, 686:2.
12. Talmud, Taanit 30b.
13. Talmud, Taanit 26b.
14. R. Yosef Karo, *Shulhan Arukh*, Orah Hayyim, 612, 613, 614.
15. *ibid.*, 615.
16. Leviticus, 23:32.
17. R. Yosef Karo, *Shulhan Arukh*, Orah Hayyim, 611:2.
18. Isaiah, 58:5.
19. Maimonides, *Mishnah Torah*, Laws of Repentance, 2:1–2; 6–7.
20. *ibid.*, 2:4.
21. Leviticus, 12:3.
22. R. Yosef Karo, *Shulhan Arukh*, Yore Deah, 263:4.
23. Leviticus, 12:3.
24. Reason suggested by R. Avraham Yitzhak Sperling, in his *Taamay Ha-Minhagim*, no. 910. (Sephardic custom is to recite this blessing at a circumcision.)
25. *ibid.*, no. 922.
26. James J. Lynch, *The Broken Heart: The Medical Consequences of Loneliness* (New York: Basic Books, 1979), pp. 169–170.
27. Genesis, 1:28; 9:7.
28. Genesis, 3:16.
29. See commentary of R. Samson Raphael Hirsch, who connects the notion of giving birth in agony with the idea that happiness comes by way of sacrifice.
30. Hirsch's translation.
31. Talmud, Yevamot 65b.
32. R. Yosef Karo, *Shulhan Arukh*, Even HaEzer, 1:5. This is based on the notion that the fulfillment of a precept accrues only to the individual who is obliged to fulfill the precept.
33. *ibid.*, 1:13. See further, R. Yosef Epstein, *Sefer Mitzvot HaBayit* (New York: Torat Ha'Adam Institute, 1975), chapter 1, "HaIsh V'Ishto," pp. 81–84.
34. See further, Reuven P. Bulka, *Jewish Marriage: A Halakhic Ethic* (Hoboken, New Jersey: Ktav Publishing House, 1986), ca. end of chapter 2.

35. See gloss of R. Moshe Isserles to R. Yosef Karo, *Shulhan Arukh*, Yore Deah, 251:3, who states that providing for one's self comes before providing for anyone else and one is not obliged to give charity until one has enough for one's self.
36. R. Yosef Karo, *Shulhan Arukh*, Even HaEzer, 1:5 and 5.
37. *ibid.*, Yore Deah, 263:1–2.
38. Talmud, Berakhot 17a.
39. Talmud, Berakhot 5b.
40. Talmud, Baba Mezia 85a.
41. Talmud, Berakhot 5a.
42. Talmud, Shabbat 55a.
43. Talmud, Bezah 32b.
44. Talmud, Avot 4:19.
45. Talmud, Taanit 8a.
46. Talmud, Arakhin 16b. Even placing the hand into one's pocket to take out three coins and only two come up is considered in the general framework of suffering.
47. Talmud, Berakhot 54a.
48. Talmud, Berakhot 60b. See also R. Yosef Karo, *Shulhan Arukh*, Orah Hayyim, 222:1.
49. Talmud, Berakhot 60b. Also R. Yosef Karo, *Shulhan Arukh*, Orah Hayyim, 222:2, 3. The irony is that accepting gracefully the unavoidable bad that befalls the self is a way of serving God; this in itself is a joy.
50. Talmud, Avot 6:4.
51. See Reuven P. Bulka, *As a Tree by the Waters—Pirkey Avoth: Psychological and Philosophical Insights* (New York: Feldheim, 1980), pp. 248–249.

CHAPTER 4: COUNTERING DEPRESSION

1. There are the normal occasional ups and downs, what are referred to as the "blues;" also situations depressing by their very nature—being fired from one's job, taking a heavy loss on an investment, or suffering a much more vital loss—of a loved one.
2. Talmud, Shabbat 30b.
3. R. Yosef Karo, *Shulhan Arukh*, Orah Hayyim, 1:1; 6:3.
4. Talmud, Berakhot 31a.
5. Talmud, Eruvin 65b.
6. *ibid.*

7. Leviticus, 19:18.
8. Hirsch's rendition is as follows: "Love thy neighbour's well-being as 'twere thine own."
9. Exodus, 20:13.
10. See Reuven P. Bulka, "Rabbinic Attitudes Towards Suicide," in Reuven P. Bulka and Moshe HaLevi Spero (Eds.), *A Psychology-Judaism Reader* (Springfield, Illinois: Charles C. Thomas, 1982), pp. 211–225.
11. Biblically, there is no legislated punishment for attempted murder. The courts were, of course, empowered to take any steps necessary to maintain societal equilibrium.
12. Midrash Rabbah, Leviticus, 13:3.
13. Talmud, Makkot 23b.
14. Talmud, Kiddushin 40b.
15. R. Yosef Karo, *Shulhan Arukh*, Orah Hayyim, 529:6. See R. Yisrael Meir HaKohen, in *Mishnah Brurah* 529, Note 11. See also Maimonides, *Mishnah Torah*, Laws of the Festivals, 6:16. This also applies to Shabbat. See Maimonides, *loc. cit.*, Laws of Shabbat, 30:10.
16. Maimonides, *loc. cit.*, Laws of the Festivals, 6:18.
17. Deuteronomy, 24:5.
18. Talmud, Avot 1:14.
19. Talmud, Eruvin 13b.
20. R. Yosef Karo, *Shulhan Arukh*, Orah Hayyim, 493.
21. The Fast of the 9th of Av, and the 3 weeks preceding it, actually commemorate the destruction of both Temples.
22. Talmud, Rosh Hashanah 18b.
23. R. Yosef Karo, *Shulhan Arukh*, Orah Hayyim, 551:2,4,9.
24. See *ibid.*, entire section 551.
25. *ibid.*, 554:1.
26. *ibid.*, 554:20.
27. Talmud, Taanit 30b.
28. Jerusalem Talmud, Berakhot 2:4.
29. Talmud, Berakhot 31a.
30. Talmud, Taanit 22a.
31. Psalms, 100:2.

Chapter 5: Experiencing Pleasure

1. Ecclesiastes, 8:15.
2. Ecclesiastes, 2:2.
3. Talmud, Shabbat 30b.

4. Talmud, Avot 3:17.
5. Jerusalem Talmud, Sukkah 5:1.
6. Talmud, Avot 4:1.
7. *ibid.*, 3:16.
8. *ibid.*, 2:17.
9. Psalms, 100:2.
10. R. Yosef Karo, *Shulhan Arukh*, Orah Hayyim, 554:1.
11. *ibid.*, and also 2–4.
12. Psalms, 19:9.
13. Talmud, Yevamot 20a: "Sanctify yourself in that which is permitted to you."
14. Talmud, Moed Katan 8b.
15. R. Yosef Karo, *Shulhan Arukh*, Orah Hayyim, 546:1.
16. Talmud, Sanhedrin 24b.
17. *ibid.*, and R. Yosef Karo, *Shulhan Arukh*, Hoshen Mishpat, 34:16,17.
18. Talmud, Pesahim 109a.
19. Talmud, Sanhedrin 70a.
20. Talmud, Yoma 76b.
21. Talmud, Eruvin 65a.
22. Talmud, Pesahim 42b.
23. *ibid.*, 42a.
24. Talmud, Ketuvot 65b.
25. Talmud, Shabbat 111a.
26. Midrash Rabbah, Numbers, 10:6.
27. Midrash Rabbah, Leviticus, 12:4.
28. See Talmud, Sotah 2a.
29. Talmud, Gittin 70a.
30. Psalms, 104:15.
31. Talmud, Sanhedrin 70a.
32. Talmud, Pesahim 106a.
33. R. Yosef Karo, *Shulhan Arukh*, Even HaEzer, 62:1.
34. *loc. cit.*, Yore Deah, 265:1.
35. *ibid.*, 305:8.
36. Talmud, Pesahim 99b.
37. Jerusalem Talmud, Pesahim 10:1.
38. Leviticus, 10:9.
39. Talmud, Sanhedrin 83b.
40. Talmud, Keritut 13b. See Maimonides, *Mishnah Torah*, Laws of Entry into the Sanctuary, 1:1–2, that only wine-induced drunkenness is a capital offence, whereas with other intoxicants there is a prohibition but it is not of capital import.

41. Psalms, 100:2.
42. Psalms, 104:15.
43. Exodus, 19:6.
44. Leviticus, 10:10.
45. Genesis, 28:12.
46. Talmud, Berakhot 31b.
47. Genesis, 9:5. See related discussion in chapter 2, of this title, in sections titled "Modern Application," and "Avoiding Danger."
48. R. Yosef Karo, *Shulhan Arukh*, Hoshen Mishpat, 427.
49. Deuteronomy, 4:9.
50. *ibid.*, 4:15. See R. Yosef Karo, *Shulhan Arukh*, Orah Hayyim, 571.
51. See Maimonides, *Mishnah Torah*, Laws of the Murderer and Self-Preservation, Chapters 11 and 12, for the host of restrictions involving self-preservation.
52. *ibid.*, 11:5. See, in this title, chapter 4, section on "Two Sides of Life."
53. Psalms, 116:6; Talmud, Shabbat 129b, Niddah 31a.
54. R. Moshe Feinstein, *Igrot Moshe* (New York: Balshon, 1973), Yore Deah 2, 49.
55. J. David Bleich, "Survey of Recent Halakhic Periodical Literature: Smoking," in *Tradition: A Journal of Orthodox Jewish Thought*, Summer 1977, *16(4)*, 121–123.
56. Talmud, Ketuvot 111a.

CHAPTER 6: ENJOYMENT OF LIFE

1. Talmud, Shabbat 133b.
2. Leviticus, 23:40.
3. R. Yosef Karo, *Shulhan Arukh*, Orah Hayyim, 648.
4. *ibid.*, 639:1.
5. Exodus, 25:10–11.
6. Talmud, Baba Batra 4a.
7. Medicine was one of the few fields where the restrictions placed upon the Jewish community did not hold. In many instances, the Jewish community set up its own medical school for the training of doctors.
8. See for example, Talmud, Avodah Zarah 44a–44b. Also, R. Yosef Karo, *Shulhan Arukh*, Yore Deah, 141:4,7.
9. See further on this, Cecil Roth, *The Jewish Contribution to Civilization* (Cincinnati: Union of American Hebrew Congregations, 1940), pp. 146–149.
10. See *ibid.* The art of this generation is a reference to the works of such as Agam.

11. R. Yosef Karo, *Shulhan Arukh*, Orah Hayyim, 228.

12. *ibid.*, 226.

13. *ibid.*, 225:10.

14. *ibid.*

15. *ibid.*, 426:1.

16. *ibid.*, 229:2

17. *ibid.*, 227:1.

18. *ibid.*, 229:1.

19. Talmud, Avot 3:9.

20. This is reported in Martin Gordon, "A Fullness of Life," in *Journal of Jewish Thought* (New York: Rabbinical Council of America, 1985), pp. 123–124.

21. R. Yosef Karo, *Shulhan Arukh*, Orah Hayyim, 225:10.

22. *ibid.*, 224:7,8.

23. Talmud, Avodah Zarah 20a.

24. R. Yosef Karo, *Shulhan Arukh*, Even HaEzer, 21:1,3. Also, Maimonides, *Mishnah Torah*, Laws of Forbidden Intercourse, 21:2.

25. Talmud, Nedarim 20a. Also, R. Yosef Karo, *Shulhan Arukh*, Orah Hayyim, 240:4, and Maimonides, *Mishnah Torah*, Laws of Forbidden Intercourse, 21:9.

26. For example, Exodus, 15:1–21; Deuteronomy, 32:1–43; Judges, 5:1–31; II Samuel, 22:2–51.

27. II Kings, 3:15.

28. Related to R. Yosef Karo, *Shulhan Arukh*, Yore Deah, 391:1–2, which prohibits any joy, and music fits into that category.

29. See R. Yosef Karo, *Shulhan Arukh*, Orah Hayyim, 493, on the host of restrictions during the period between Passover and Pentecost.

30. *ibid.*, 560:3.

31. Talmud, Arakhin 11a. The Talmud there asserts that the notion of service in joy and with a good heart refers to song.

32. Cecil Roth, *op. cit.*, 161–171.

33. Talmud, Ketuvot 59b.

34. *ibid.*

35. Exodus, 20:8–11; Avot D'Rabbe Natan 11:1.

36. See Reuven P. Bulka, "The Role of the Individual in Jewish Law," in *Tradition: A Journal of Orthodox Jewish Thought*, Spring/Summer 1973, *13:4–14:1*, 124–136.

37. Talmud, Rosh Hashanah 27a; Shavuot 20b.

38. Talmud, Sanhedrin 108a.

39. See the elaboration on this subject in the commentary of R. Samson Raphael Hirsch to Genesis, 8:22.

40. Genesis, 8:22.
41. The Talmud, Berakhot 57b, speaks of those things that enlarge the spirit of the individual, giving him a sense of equanimity. Among these are a pleasant home and a pleasant wife. Obviously, in an individual's leisure time, it is very congenial to have a pleasant environment, engender a good relationship with one's spouse, and have a happy home atmosphere.
42. Talmud, Avot 3:14.

CHAPTER 7: PLEASURES OF THE PALATE

1. *Deuteronomy, 14:11, 20.
2. See Leviticus, 11:4–7, for use of the term *tamai*. On exemption in life-threatening situations, see Talmud, Yoma 85b and Sanhedrin 74a.
3. Leviticus, 11:3.
4. Leviticus, 11:13–19.
5. Leviticus, 11:9–10.
6. Talmud, Hullin 27b, based on numbers 11:22. See also R. Yosef Karo, *Shulhan Arukh*, Yore Deah, 13:1.
7. See R. Aharon of Barcelona, *Sefer HaHinukh*, nos. 73, 147, and 154.
8. See commentary of Nahmanides to Leviticus 11:13.
9. *ibid.*, 11:10. Of course, the dietary regulations, like the other precepts, stand on their own. The health connection merely reinforces the view that biblical legislation is intended to enhance the human being rather than to harm or stifle.
10. Talmud, Hullin 109b.
11. *ibid.*
12. Jerusalem Talmud, Kiddushin 4:12.
13. Talmud, Hullin 28a.
14. R. Yosef Karo, *Shulhan Arukh*, Yore Deah, 1:1.
15. The terminology employed in the Talmud is *talmid-hakham*, which translates as student scholar. The true scholar always was a student because the true scholar knew there was always more to learn. Thus was fused the notion of intellectual curiosity with appropriate humility.
16. R. Yosef Karo, *Shulhan Arukh*, Yore Deah, 18:2.
17. *ibid.*, 23:2.
18. *ibid.*, 24:7.
19. See Talmud, Pesahim 109a.
20. Deuteronomy, 12:20. See Talmud, Hullin 84a.
21. Avot D'Rabbe Natan, 26:5. See Chapter 2 in this title, section on "Some Rules."

22. Talmud, Kiddushin 40b. See R. Yosef Karo, *Shulhan Arukh*, Hoshen Mishpat, 34:18, where it is contemplated that such an individual is actually unfit to serve as a witness.

23. Talmud, Gittin 70a; Derekh Eretz Rabbah, 6:5.

24. See Proverbs, 13:25, that the righteous eat to satisfy their souls, whereas the bellies of the wicked are always deficient. That verse may in fact be linked to the difference between eating as a glutton, and eating respectfully and in dignity, as do the righteous.

25. Talmud, Shabbat 129b.

26. Talmud, Gittin 70a.

27. Avot D'Rabbe Natan, 28:9.

28. Talmud, Shabbat 25b. On this, see Chapter 2 of this title, section on "Hygiene."

29. Talmud, Shabbat 33a.

30. Talmud, Yoma 74b.

31. Talmud, Yoma 75b.

32. Talmud, Berakhot 40a.

33. Talmud, Sanhedrin 17b and Eruvin 55b.

34. Midrash on Psalms, 30:1.

35. Talmud, Gittin 69b; also Baba Mezia 107b.

36. Talmud, Baba Batra 12b.

37. Numbers, 11:4.

38. *ibid.*, 11:20.

39. Midrash Rabbah, Genesis, 9:12.

40. Talmud, Berakhot 35a.

41. Talmud, Berakhot 21a. See also, for example, R. Yosef Karo, *Shulhan Arukh*, Orah Hayyim, 208.

42. Psalms, 24:1.

43. Psalms, 115:16.

44. Berakhot, 35a-b.

45. Talmud, Taanit, 11a.

46. *ibid.* See also discussions in first chapter in this title, section on "Judaism on Denial." Also in this title, chapter 3, section on "Defining Pain."

47. Deuteronomy, 8:10.

48. This is a rephrasing of the Talmudic statement that if, as has been established, there is a biblical obligation to recite a blessing *after* one has eaten, then it is eminently logical that one should be obliged to recite a blessing *before* one has eaten.

49. As per the verse in Proverbs, 13:25, that the righteous eat to satisfy their souls. They eat in order to be able to serve; the eating is elevated to a spiritually significant endeavor.

50. Talmud, Avot 3:4.
51. Ezekiel, 41:22.
52. *ibid.*

CHAPTER 8: SENSUAL PLEASURE

1. Talmud, Berakhot 61a; Eruvin, 18a.
2. Leviticus, 18:22 and 20:13.
3. Leviticus, 18:3. See R. Yosef Karo, *Shulhan Arukh, Even HaEzer* 20:2. Also, Maimonides, *Mishnah Torah,* Laws of Forbidden Intercourse, 21:18.
4. See Midrash Tanhuma, Tazria, 11: "Through what are plagues visited? Through harlotry." Sexually transmitted diseases, according to projections, will afflict one-quarter of the American population.
5. See Deuteronomy, 33:4, that the entire corpus of Torah Law is referred to as an inheritance of the entire congregation of Yaakov; it is addressed to the community, and it is through adherence that community is forged. See also Talmud, Avot 2:5.
6. Talmud, Niddah 13a. The Talmud condemns this as a crime of capital import.
7. See R. Avraham Ben David, *Ba'aley HaNefesh,* Shaar Hakedushah, where he suggests that conjugality during pregnancy is the second most exalted level of sexual expression.
8. Leviticus, 18:6–18.
9. See, for example, Leviticus, 18:20. See further Reuven P. Bulka, *Jewish Marriage: A Halakhic Ethic* (Hoboken, New Jersey: Ktav Publishing House, 1986), Note 42 to Chapter 3.
10. Maimonides, *Guide for the Perplexed,* 3:49.
11. See Reuven P. Bulka, "Divorce: The Problem and the Challenge," *Tradition: A Journal of Orthodox Jewish Thought,* Summer 1976, *16:1,* 127–133.
12. Further on this, see Moshe HaLevi Spero, *Judaism and Psychology: Halakhic Perspectives* (New York: Ktav Publishing House and Yeshiva University Press, 1980), pp. 64–81.
13. Deuteronomy, 6:5.
14. Talmud, Berakhot 54a.
15. Midrash Rabbah, Genesis, 9:9.
16. Talmud, Avot 4:1.
17. Talmud, Sukkah 52b.
18. *ibid.,* 52a.

19. *ibid.*, 52b.
20. See Reuven P. Bulka, *Jewish Marriage: A Halakhic Ethic* (Hoboken, New Jersey: Ktav Publishing House, 1986), especially Chapters 10 and 11.
21. Proverbs, 18:22.
22. R. Yehudah HaHasid, *Sefer Hasidim*, no. 509.
23. Talmud, Avot 5:19.
24. II Samuel, 13:15.
25. See Reuven P. Bulka, *The Quest For Ultimate Meaning: Principles and Applications of Logotherapy* (New York: Philosophical Library, 1979), pp. 151–163.
26. Talmud, Yoma 74b speaks of the affliction of separation.
27. Talmud, Sotah 11b.
28. Talmud, Shabbat 140b.
29. Talmud, Eruvin 100b.
30. See further, Reuven P. Bulka, *Jewish Marriage: A Halakhic Ethic* (Hoboken, New Jersey: Ktav Publishing House, 1986), especially Chapters 10 and 11.
31. Talmud, Eruvin 100b.
32. R. Yosef Karo, *Shulhan Arukh*, Orah Hayyim, 240:15. Also, Maimonides, *Mishnah Torah*, Laws of Opinions, 5:4.
33. Talmud, Nedarim 20b. Also, R. Yosef Karo, *Shulhan Arukh*, Even Ha-Ezer, 25:9 and Maimonides, *Mishnah Torah*, Laws of Forbidden Intercourse, 21:12.
34. The scope of the regulations is well set forth in R. Yosef Karo, *Shulhan Arukh*, Yore Deah, Chapters 183 to 200.
35. See Chapter 7 of this title, section on "Overindulgence."
36. Talmud, Niddah 31b.
37. R. Yosef Karo, *Shulhan Arukh*, Even HaEzer, 76:11, and Maimonides, *Mishnah Torah*, Laws of Marital Relationships, 14:7.
38. R. Yosef Karo, *Shulhan Arukh*, Even HaEzer, 76:4.
39. Statement of R. Avraham Ben David, in *Ba'aley HaNefesh*, Shaar HaKedushah.
40. R. Yosef Karo, *Shulhan Arukh*, Orah Hayyim, 240:1 and Even HaEzer, 76:1,2. Also, Maimonides, *Mishnah Torah*, Laws of Marital Relationships, 14:1.
41. Talmud, Nedarim 20b. Also, R. Yosef Karo, *Shulhan Arukh*, Even Ha-Ezer, 25:2. Also Maimonides, *Mishnah Torah*, Laws of Forbidden Intercourse, 21:12.
42. See the Talmud, Pesahim 72; one is obligated to make one's wife happy via the conjugal command.

43. Exodus, 21:10. See also Chapter 3 of this title, section on "Procreation and Labor Pains."
44. R. Yosef Karo, *Shulhan Arukh*, Even HaEzer, 77:1–2. Also, Maimonides, *Mishnah Torah*, Laws of Marital Relationships, 14:6–8.
45. Talmud, Niddah 71a.
46. Talmud, Gittin 70a.
47. Talmud, Nedarim 20b.
48. Talmud, Niddah 16b, 17a. See too, R. Yosef Karo, *Shulhan Arukh*, Orah Hayyim, 240:11 and Even HaEzer, 25:5, as well as Maimonides, *Mishnah Torah*, Laws of Forbidden Intercourse, 21:10.
49. Talmud, Nedarim 20a and R. Yosef Karo, *Shulhan Arukh*, Orah Hayyim, 240:4. But see Even HaEzer, 25:2, and Maimonides, *Mishnah Torah*, Laws of Forbidden Intercourse, 21:9.
50. See Reuven P. Bulka, *Jewish Marriage: A Halakhic Ethic* (Hoboken, New Jersey: Ktav Publishing House, 1986), Note 25 to Chapter 11.
51. In a work attributed by some to Nahmanides, *The Holy Letter*, Chapter 2, the statement is made that when the husband-wife conjugal union is for heaven's sake, nothing is more holy or pure.
52. Talmud, Berakhot 62a.

CHAPTER 9: CONCLUSION

1. Talmud, Avot 1:14.
2. The observation is made by Raphael Patai, in *The Jewish Mind* (New York: Scribner's, 1977), pp. 502–504.
3. Talmud, Taanit 11a.
4. *ibid*.
5. R. Yosef Karo, *Shulhan Arukh*, Orah Hayyim, 560:2.
6. Ecclesiastes, 3:4.
7. Deuteronomy, 6:7. Also, Talmud, Berakhot 10b.
8. There was in fact only one prohibition, as per Genesis, 2:17.
9. Genesis, 3:19.
10. Genesis, 3:17.
11. Genesis, 3:16.
12. Psalms, 128:2.
13. Talmud, Makkot 23b.
14. Deuteronomy, 30:15.
15. Deuteronomy, 30:19.

Index